MODERN NEPAL

BY THE SAME AUTHOR

Rise of Nepal and Bhutan, 1984
Royal Bhutan, 1983
Struggle for Central Asia, 1982
Modern Central Asia, 1979
The Himalaya as a Frontier, 1978
Politics of Central Asia, 1972
Modern Bhutan, 1971
The Himalaya Borderland, 1970
Government and Politics of Tibet, 1969

His Majesty King Birendra Bir Bikram Dev Shah

MODERN NEPAL

Ram Rahul

Jawaharlal Nehru University

Munshiram Manoharlal
Publishers Pvt. Ltd.

First published 1985

PRINTED IN INDIA

PUBLISHED BY MUNSHIRAM MANOHARLAL PUBLISHERS PVT. LTD., POST BOX 5715, 54 RANI JHANSI ROAD, NEW DELHI 110055 AND PRINTED BY PRAMODH KAPUR AT RAJ BANDHU INDUSTRIAL CO., C-61, MAYAPURI, PHASE II, NEW DELHI 110064

Contents

Preface

Nepal is the ancient land of an ancient people. It lies on the southern slopes of the Central Himalaya, and adjoins China and India. In ancient times, Nepal was one of the kingdoms of India's Himalaya frontiers like Pragjyotisha/Kamarupa (present-day Assam), Brahmapura (present-day Garhwal and Kumaun), Kuluta (present-day Kulu) and Kashmir. However, until the second half of the eighteenth century, or until 1768-69 to be precise, the name "Nepal" denoted only the valley of the Bagmati River, where Kathmandu, the present capital of modern Nepal, is situated. The modern period of Nepal begins with the conquest of the kingdoms of the Bagmati Valley by Prithvinarayan Shah of Gorkha in 1768–69.

Modern Nepal deals with Nepal of the post 1769 period. Next I study the period of the kings of the whole of Nepal. Modern Nepal consists of three distinct periods, viz 1769-1846, 1846-1951 and 1951. I start with the survey of the history of Nepal up to 1769. The kings of Nepal both reigned and ruled absolutely in the first period, which was also a period of tremendous court intrigue. A certain family of the Thapa clan emerged to political power in Nepal after a bloody coup, known as the "Kot" massacre, in 1846. The Rana prime ministers enjoyed enormous powers. Indeed they can be said to have been *de facto* kings of Nepal in the second period from 1846 to 1951. The overthrow of the Rana oligarchy in 1951 resulted in the restoration of the monarchy to its original position of power and supremacy in Nepalese affairs. The kings of the third period from 1951 to date have ruled with the help of advisers, or democratically, or directly. Then I quickly survey Nepalese Hinduism which has had a great hearing on Nepalese history and culture. After this I study Nepal's relations with its neighbours especially China and India. I conclude the study with certain projections on the future of Nepal on the basis of its history and politics.

The Bibliography lists only certain works on Nepal in English and Nepali. I have omitted all works on Nepal published in languages which I do not use. The Appendices contain only select documents.

I dedicate this study to the fond memory of Dr S.N Mitter, who took care of my eyes and thereby enabled me to write my books. I must also make grateful mention here of the kind concern shown by Dr Hari Mohan for the health of my eyes. I thank the officials of the Royal Government of Nepal for their many courtesies. I am also thankful to Lt. Governor M.L. Kampani of the Andamans (Port Blair) and Vice-Chancellor D.B. Dutta of the University of North Bengal (Siliguri, District Darjeeling) for their gracious interest in this study on Nepal. My thanks are further due to S.S. Deora of the School of International Studies, Jawaharlal Nehru University, New Delhi, for his help in the preparation of the manuscript of this study.

Ram Rahul

School of International Studies
Jawaharlal Nehru University
New Delhi 110 067

CHAPTER 1

Historical Perspective

NEPAL is an ancient land. Its heritage is splendid. The history of Nepal goes back to the establishment of the political authority of the Kirat tribes. According to a Nepalese tradition, Emperor Ashoka visited Patan, one of the kingdoms of the Bagmati Valley, around 250 B.C. According to the monk-historian Taranatha of Tibet, Ashoka subdued the Khasas and the people of Nepal, who had revolted. The *Prashasti* pillar inscription of Samudragupta at Allahabad describes ancient Nepal as a frontier kingdom of India like Pragjyotisha (ancient Assam), Brahampura (ancient Kumaun and Garhwal), Kashmir, etcetra. It remained within the cultural world of India even after its political detachment from India. China had no connection with Nepal in the ancient time. Visits of Chinese or Nepalis to each other's country are mere episodes historically whatever Chinese or Nepalese political nationalism may make of them now.

The Lichchhavis, who moved from the Mahabharat region in the south to Nepal of the Bagmati Valley around the third century A.D., ruled Nepal from the first half of the fourth century A.D. to the second half of the eighth. According to the pillar inscription, in the Changunarayan temple near Kathmandu, of the latter half of the fifth century A.D. the Lichchhavi Raja Manadeva (*c.r.* 464-595) was the first powerful monarch of ancient

Nepal. He firmly suppressed the *samanta* feudatories and extended his domain up to the Gandaki River in the west. He had his kingly title inscribed on the Changunarayan pillar.

Manadeva's successors particularly Raja Shivadeva (*c.r.* 595-623) not being strong enough, their *mahasamanta* high feudatories took much of the power in their own hands. Amshuvarman, a Thakuri mahasamanta, took all power for himself. He even assumed the title of Maharaja. He married Raja Shivadeva's daughter.

The reign of Amshuvarman is one of the brightest periods in the history of ancient Nepal. The large number of coins and inscriptions of Amshuvarman, and the account of Nepal written by Hsuan Tsang (who was at Vaishali, North Bihar, north of the Ganga in *c.* 637, when Amshuvarman was already dead) speak highly of Amshuvarman's administrative and literary genius. Suppression of the unruly feudatories and tribal chiefs was one of his achievements. The nature of his relations with Tibet, which had just entered upon its empire building phase under King Srongtsen Gampo (*r.* 627-49), the first historical king of ancient Tibet, is rather obscure. The admission of Hsuan Tsang and the Chinese annals of the T'ang dynasty (618-908) respecting Amshuvarman's independent status, however, dispel any doubt about his acceptance of Tibetan suzerainty. The Nepalese historical tradition also does not admit the fact of Tibetan domination over Nepal even though Narendradeva (*r.* 645-81), son and successor of Raja Udayadeva and grandson of Raja Shivadeva, is said to have succeeded on the throne of Nepal with the help of Srongtsen Gampo. Anyway Nepal exercised a strong cultural influence on Tibet through Buddhism and its own artistic idioms. Whatsoever, with the growth of close relations between

Nepal and Tibet, the former became well known to China as well.

Adi Shankaracharya (*c.* 788-820) set up a *matha* (Hindu monastery) on the west bank of the Bagmati River and made regular arrangements for worship of Lord Pashupati. Tradition has always required, and requires priests of the temple of Pashupati to come from South India, from Gokarna on the coast halfway between Goa and Mangalore. The King of Nepal on his part shares with the Shankaracharyas of Puri, Shringeri and Rameshwaram the right to worship in the sanctums of Puri, Shringeri and Rameshwaram.

Dipankara Srijnana of the Vikramashila monastic university, Atisha of the Tibetan tradition, visited Nepal on his way to Tibet towards the end of the reign of Raja Lakshmikamadeva (*r.* 1024-41) in the summer of 1041. He introduced the tantrik version of Mahayana Buddhism in Nepal.

The Thakuri dynasty went into oblivion during the reign of Raja Gunakamadeva. One Ari Malla founded the Malla dynasty (1201-1769). The Mallas were from the Tarai plains of the Kushinagar region of present-day Uttar Pradesh of India. With them began the medieval period of Nepal.

After subduing Tirhut, Shamsuddin Ilyas of Lakhnauti/Gouda (present-day Western Bengal) raided Nepal and plundered, looted and ransacked its shrines and temples in 1334. Jayasimha Malla, a feudatory from Banepa, restored the Pashupati Temple.

From a background obscured by this chaos, Jayasthiti Malla (1360-95) emerged as one of the most notable rulers of medieval Nepal. His position became specially strong after the death of Raja Jayarjun Malla (*r.* 1361-82). Tradition remembers Raja Jayasthiti Malla as a patron of literature and as the initiator of many social and economic reforms in the country. He reorganized the Nepalese, Newar society, defining the status of different castes according to *Manusmriti*, the code of Manu, and fixing them on the basis of professions and functions. He also maintained friendly relations with his neighbours, thereby enhancing the prestige of the country.

Raja Jayayaksha Malla (*r.* 1428-72), grandson of Raja Jayasthiti Malla, combined all the kingdoms of the Bagmati Valley into the Malla kingdom of Nepal, the boundaries of which extended up to Tibet in the north, Gorkha in the west and Morang in the south—the farthest limits that the Malla domain ever gained. But the division of his kingdom among his three sons (his sons Raya Malla, Ran Malla and Ratna Malla ruled Bhadgau (modern Bhatgau), Banepa and Kathmandu and his daughter Dharmawati ruled Patan) in 1482 eventually led to the fall of the Malla dynasty in 1768-69, when Raja Prithvinarayan Shah of Gorkha conquered all the Malla kingdoms of the Bagmati Valley.

Nepal before 1769 thus is not representative of the whole of Nepal as it is understood today. There also were a number of other principalities in the Central Himalaya in addition to those of the Bagmati Valley. On the eve of the rise of the house of Gorkha in 1559, the other main centres of power between the Mechi and the Kali rivers, which mark the eastern and western limits of Nepal today, were the chiefs of the Kirat tribe (Limbu and Rai septs) of the Arun Valley, the kings of the Sen dynasty of the Tarai and the *Chhogyal*/King of Sukhim (anglicized Sikkim) in the east as well as the *Choubisi Rajya*, the confederation of the twenty-four principalities of the Gandaki basin like Tanahun, Palpa, Parbat, Lamjung, Kaski, Bhirkot, etc. and the *Baisi Rajya*, the confederation of the twenty-two principalities of the Karnali basin like Pyuthan, Sallyan, Jajarkot, Jumla, Doti, Bajhang, etc. in the west and the *Gyalpo*/King of Mustang in the north. Pyuthan was the eastern most of the Baisi region. East of it was the Choubisi region. Although the numbers may have been more or less, the terms remained traditional for the two groups of the federated principalities.

The history of most of these principalities is still obscure. The principalities in the Eastern, Central and Western Tarai had developed from the pre-British parts of Bengal, Bihar and Uttar Pradesh along the foothills. The principalities in the Eastern Tarai were under the rule of Sen princes who had fled from the plains of India to escape the reach of the Muslim rulers. The Baisi and the Choubisi domains were under Rajput princes descended from those who had fled from the plains of India into the hills of the Central, Western Himalaya in the thirteenth and fourteenth centuries.

Before the Gorkha conquest of Doti in 1785, all the Baisi domains, including Jumla, the oldest, largest and most prominent principality among the Baisi confederation, recognized the superiority of Kumaun. The Raja of Bajhang used to ascend the throne only after receiving the robe of honour from the Maharaja of Kumaun. The Maharaja of Kumaun in his turn recognized the supremacy of the Mughal emperor of Delhi. All the Baisi and Choubisi rulers thus owed allegiance to the Mughal emperor in Delhi. The arm of Mughal imperial authority, however, was never long enough to control them effectively. As the Mughal power declined, the intractable hill potentates emerged altogether independent.

CHAPTER 2

Nepal 1769-75

AFTER conquering the Malla kingdoms of the Bagmati Valley in 1768-69, Prithvinarayan Shah set out to take the other centres of power in the Central Himalaya east and west of Kathmandu. In view of the rapidly spreading British domain towards the Himalaya frontier countries then, especially the Eastern Tarai, he first moved towards the east and the south. According to his perception, British advance threatened the security of Nepal created by him. Perhaps no centre of power in the west posed that kind of a threat to him. His native Gorkha itself was one of those centres. He also had social relations with them. He himself was the son of Maharani Kaushalya, the daughter of the Raja of Palpa. He gave his own daughter from his first wife Indrakumari, the daughter of Raja Hem Karn Sen of Makwanpur, in marriage to the Raja of Sallyan. He conducted diplomatic correspondence with not a few of them, but he was in no hurry to weld them into the fabric of his Nepal.

Prithvinarayan Shah thus viewed campaigning in the east as much more important than campaigning in the west. His armies built a number of forts both to facilitate the eastern march and to secure communications with the plains in the south. They conquered the Sen domain of Choudandi in early 1774. On the death of Raja Karn Sen of Choudandi in the battle, his brother Budhi Karpo Sen escaped to Morang. The territories of

Choudandi lay in the hills as well as the plains. Ilam also fell to the Gorkhas. Morang with its capital Vijayapur extended up to the Teesta River in the east and bordered Sikkim. The Kankai Mai/Lha Chhu, which in its upper reaches flows to the east of Ilam then formed the boundary between Morang and Sikkim With the capture of Changthapu and Islimba, south of Ilam, Prithvinarayan Shah's domains in the east became contiguous with those of the *Sikkimpati*, the Lord of Sikkim. *Sardar* (Military Commander) Ramkrishna Kanwar was the general of the Choudandi campaign. Amar Singh Thapa, a young officer of the Choudandi campaign, won extensive victories under the successors of Prithvinarayan Shah.

For the support Prithvinarayan Shah received from the chiefs of the fiercely independent Limbus and Rais flanking his armies, he allowed them to continue with their *kipat* system of community land tenure and assured them internal autonomy under their own chiefs. Prithvinarayan Shah had annexed the Kirat land, present Limbuana, shortly before his death.

Prithvinarayan Shah had already in 1762 taken Makwanpur, the second largest kingdom in the Nepal Himalaya. The misunderstanding between Raja Digbandhan Sen of Makwanpur and Prithvinarayan Shah went back to 1736/37, when the former had slighted the latter as unworthy of the hand of his sister Princess Indrakumari in marriage. Prithvinarayan was the first Gorkha prince to marry a bride from outside the hills. Digbandhan Sen's siding with Jayaprakash Malla of Kathmandu against Prithvinarayan in the 1760s impelled him to dispatch *Kajis* (Ministers) Kehar Singh, Basnyat (modern spelling Basnet) and Vanshraj Pande under the command of his brothers Mahodamkirti Shah and Dalpati Shah to attack Makwanpur. On his defeat

Digbandhan Sen escaped to the British territory.

The Gorkhas brought Indrakumari along with them. Prithvinarayan Shah always kept her at his native Gorkha. Of course, he accorded her the status of *choutara* or *choutariyal*/collateral member of the royal family. She was the second female member of the royal house of Gorkha to receive that status in the history of modern Nepal. Maharani Chandraprabhawati, senior step-mother and regent of Prithvinarayan Shah, was the first female *choutara*. Afterwards only the male members of the royal family received this title. Since the territories of Makwanpur bordered on Bhadgau and Patan in the north and Bihar in the south, Prithvinarayan's marriage with Indrakumari of Makwanpur was a strategic one meant to develop a close alliance between Gorkha and Makwanpur. His marriage with Narendralakshmi of Varanasi was a tactical one meant to demonstrate the pride of his Rajput ancestry. His younger stepbrothers Mahodamkirti and Dalmardan also married into the same family.

Nepal now extended from Gorkha in the west to Bhutan and Sikkim in the east. Only the Baisi and the Choubisi domains remained to be taken to complete the map of present-day Nepal. The Gorkha armies completed this task in the 1780s and 1790s. Sardar Prabal Shatrudal Shahi took Achham and Doti in 1791.

The rulers of the erstwhile Baisi and Choubisi kingdoms, however, continued to enjoy their titulary status until the middle of this century. With the solitary exception of the Gyalpo of Mustang on the Tibet border, the process of the political unification and consolidation of Nepal completed in the early 1960s in accordance with King Mahendra Bir Bikram Shah's abolition of the feudal privileges of the titulary kings of Nepal vide the *Raja Rajauta Ain 2017* (Rajya Abolition Act of 1961).

With the exception of the Raja of Bajhang, who eventually escaped to Bhimtal near Nainital, the titulary rulers did not offer any resistance to King Mahendra's abolition of their privileges. On his part, King Mahendra successfully placated them by marrying his daughter Princess Shanti Devi to the son of the Raja of Bajhang and by appointing the Raja of Thalari as his ambassador to India. Bajhang has a long border with Kumaun/India. Like Mustang it also has a long border with Tibet/China. In the past it had several *thakurais* under it.

The process of unifying the numerous principalities between the Trishuli and Karnali rivers was long. Dravya Shah (*r.* 1559-70), who, according to tradition, belonged to a branch of the royal family of Chitor Garh and Udaipur and who founded the royal house of Gorkha in 1560, was the first to undertake it. Originally from Lamjung, he conquered the Magar domain of Gorkha in 1559. Later, he assumed the title of *Maharajadhiraj.*

The successors of Dravya Shah continued his work of the unification of Nepal, Ram Shah (*r.* 1609-36) enlarged his territory by conquering the neighbouring Magar chiefs. The Magars were the first tribal people of the Nepal Himalaya to adopt Hinduism. The Gurungs, the northern neighbours of the Magars, followed them. Certain Gurungs are still adherents of the Buddhism of Tibet. Ram Shah attempted to expand the Gorkha territory even towards Tibet. Anyway he is famous among the Baisi and Choubisi rulers not so much for these exploits as for his introduction of a code known as *Ram Shah ko thiti* which prescribed detailed social and administrative reforms, including weights and measures, previously unheard of in the mid-hills of the Nepal Himalaya. For this he became a celebrity among the Choubisi rulers as is evident from the saying *nyaya paune Gorkha jane* "for justice, go to Gorkha". His contemporaries addressed him as *Maharajadhiraj*. The name and term *Gorkhali*, the people of Gorkha, obtains from the time of Ram Shah.

Narbhupal Shah (*r.* 1716-42) helped the Raja of Palpa to regain Butwal from the Nawab of Awadh. He married his daughter Chandraprabhawati. When he saw that the Malla kingdoms of the Bagmati Valley were badly riven by internal feuds and factions, he attempted to conquer them. However, the garrison of the Malla frontier fortress of Nuwakot, twenty miles northwest of Kathmandu, frustrated his attack under the command of Kaji Maheshwar Pant and Jayant Rana (Magar) in 1736. Jayant Rana later went over to Raja Jayaprakash Malla (*r.* 1736-68) of Kathmandu.

When Prithvinarayan Shah succeeded his father on the throne of Gorkha on the day of Ram Navami in 1743, the kingdom of Gorkha just touched the western limits of the Bagmati Valley, although the kings of Gorkha had conquered several neighbouring hill domains and had emerged as strong rulers. He first advanced towards the Bagmati Valley. After his defeat in the first battle of Nuwakot in 1743, he strengthened his friendly relations with his neighbours especially Lamjung. Then he organized a highly disciplined army and set out to conquer the Malla kingdoms. In 1744 Mahoddamkirti, his younger step-brother, captured Nuwakot from Jayant Rana as the first step to enter the Bagmati Valley. In 1754 Prithvinarayan changed the title *Shahi*, used by the rulers of Gorkha like the other rulers of the Choubisi, to *Shah*.

Prithvinarayan Shah established his authority over Deorali, Dolkakha, Lutikot (later Balaju) and other suburban towns of the Bagmati Valley in 1750-65. He captured Kirtipur on 14 March 1766. Kathmandu fell on the day of Indrayatra-Kumariyatra on 25 September

1768 and Patan fell within seven days. By 11 November 1769, the rest of the Valley, including Bhadgau, also came under his sway. Even otherwise the Malla dynasty was on the verge of disappearance. Prithvinarayan Shah hastened the process of its extinction. Nuwakot was his headquarters from 1744 to 1769.

In response to an appeal for help from Raja Jayaprakash Malla, the government of the East India Company sought to forestall the Gorkha conquest of the Malla kingdoms by dispatching a military force under Captain W.H.D. Knox of the Bengal Army in October 1765. The British objective was to safeguard the customary trade between Bengal and Tibet through Nepal. The British expedition, however, proved fatuous. It only sowed a feeling of hostility in the Gorkha mind towards the British. All his life Prithvinarayan Shah remained suspicious of British intentions towards Nepal. He also took initiatives to form alliances with the neighbouring countries of Bhutan and Tibet to check the then expanding British power in the south. In order to maintain his friendship with Tibet, he issued very strict and clear orders to his commanders not to intrude into the territories of the *Sikkimpati*, then the protégé of Tibet.

Prithvinarayan also expelled the Jusuit missionaries and Hindu Gosains and Kashmiri Muslims from the cities of the Bagmati Valley. He suspected them to be the agents of the British commercial and other interests. The Hindu Gosains and Kashmiri Muslims carried on trade between India, Nepal and Tibet. They had *kothis* (trading houses) in Varanasi, Kathmandu and Lhasa. The successors of Prithvinarayan Shah patronized certain other non-Nepali Hindu merchants on the pattern of the *Battis kothi ka Sahu,* "merchants of thirty-two business houses", of the Malla kings of the Nepal valley.

The emergence of Prithvinarayan Shah as the supreme ruler of Nepal marked a watershed in the history not only of the Nepal Himalaya but of the entire Himalaya. Prithvinarayan Shah became the first sovereign of almost entire present-day Nepal and the house of Gorkha became its ruling dynasty. He emphasized the need of circumspection in dealing with the British in India and with the Manchus in China. His own roots lay in the history of India: he was a product of it. The Rajput Kshatriyas of India were his forebears. He described Nepal as "a yam between two stones" in its geo-political context, that is, between British India and Manchu China. He had little experience of dealing with the Manchus, but he perceived a threat to Nepal from them as they were then dominant in Tibet and could intervene in Nepal as they actually did in 1791-92. To maintain Nepal as a sovereign independent country, this imagery of Nepal as "a yam between two stones" has since provided the guideline to the makers of the Nepalese foreign policy.

All Gorkhas, regardless of rank, assumed a privileged position, a privilege based on the facts of conquest. The clans of the Gorkhas, especially their leaders, that had participated with Prithvinarayan Shah in the creation of the kingdom of Nepal became its conquest elite. From that time, too, ancestry began to be important in the Nepalese society. And so long as the Gorkhas remained the militocracy—the military elite—Nepal marched from conquest to conquest. Inspired by the feeling of patriotism infused in their hearts and minds by Prithvinarayan Shah, the Gorkhas carried their arms and pushed their conquests during 1775-1809 up to Bhutan in the east and Kangra in the west. By the end of the eighteenth century, they wielded, by means of both war and diplomacy, the congeries of the Baisi and Choubisi domains into Nepal. The Gorkha conquests included not only the Baisi and Choubisi domains but also Kumaun, Garhwal and present-day Eastern Himachal Pradesh. The Kangra-Panjab alliance, however, halted the westward advance of the Gorkhas. The Gorkhas made expansion of Nepal by military conquest the first principle of their state policy. Of course, their ambitions in the north and the south eventually brought them into conflict first with Manchu China in 1791-92 and with British India in 1814-15. Subsequently they won laurels only under the tutelage of the British. Prithvinarayan Shah is truly the founder of modern Nepal.

CHAPTER 3

Nepal 1775-1846

YUVARAJ (Heir-apparent/Crown Prince) Pratap Singh (1750-78), son of Prithvinarayan Shah from his second wife Narendralakshmi, daughter of Abhiman Singh of Varanasi, inherited a much larger kingdom than the kingdom of his forebears. He was a youngman of fine qualities. He had tantric inclinations. He devoted a lot of his time to cult and tantric pursuits. Perhaps he realized his tantric deity by consorting with his Newar wife, Maiju. On his death she became *sati*.

Maharaja Pratap Singh Shah (*r*. 1775-78) continued Prithvinarayan Shah's programme of the unification of Nepal. First the Gorkhas conquered Tanahun. The Raja of Tanahun along with Raja Virmardan Shahi of Lamjung escaped to Ram Nagar in British India. For the most part of Pratap Singh's reign, the Gorkhas engaged themselves in a war with Raja Budhi Karpo Sen of Choudandi. Pratap Singh had also intended to attack Sikkim, which then bordered on Morang. In 1777 he made a grant of *birta* land to Sardar Abhiman Singh Basnet for his successful military campaigns in the trans Arun territory, later and now known as the *Pallokirat* region, then part of Sikkim.

The Chhogyal of Sikkim exercised a tenuous authority over the Limbus and the Rais. He cultivated them through social relations, a form of control then. Generally he took one of his wives from the Limbu tribe.

Up to 1973, when Sikkim merged with India, the Limbus, known as Tsongs in Sikkim, enjoyed a privileged position in Sikkim. There have been many close kinship and social ties between them and the Lepchas.

In view of the serious skirmishes between the Gorkha and the Lepcha forces along the Arun River border in 1775, Tibet, which looked upon Sikkim as its protege, secured peace by moving Sikkim's western border further east and by making the Kankai Mai/Lha Chhu River in its upper reaches the boundary between Morang and Sikkim. Tibetan representatives, Dronyer Shalu Khenpo and Dapon Phuntshog Namyal Padtshal of Tsang, were present at the border settlement made by the Gorkhas and the Lepchas at Walong inside Sikkim territory and close to the Tibet border. According to the Tibetans, the Bhutanese had created the trouble between Nepal and Sikkim.

Yuvaraj Ran Bahadur (1775-1807) was barely two and a half years old, when he succeeded his father Pratap Singh Shah on his death in 1778. Rani Swarnaprabha was Pratap Singh Shah's other wife. A tussle for the regency between the Queen Mother/Maharani Rajendralakshmi Devi and Choutariya Bahadur Shah, led to the latter's exile to Bettiah inside the British border. However, within a few days of Rajendralakshmi Devi's death in 1785, Bahadur Shah became regent.

During the period of the regency of Choutariya Bahadur Shah from 1785 to 1794, the Gorkhas conquered the Arun territory of Sikkim in the east and took the Baisi and Choubisi domains and Kumaun in the west. The Gorkhas, however, did not annex Bajura. On the other hand, they confirmed Bajura as a feudatory domain in the summer of 1791. The Raja of Bajura had rendered valuable assistance to the Gorkhas under the command of Kaji Amar Singh Thapa, Sardar Shatrudal

Shahi and Prabal Rana respectively in their campaigns against Jumla, Doti and Achham.

The Gorkhas broke the Nepalese-Sikkimese accord in 1779. But the virile Lepchas held the Gorkhas from 1779 to 1789. Under the command of Kaji Damodar Pande, son of Kāji Kalu Pande, the Gorkhas defeated the Lepchas in a battle fought near Rabdentse, the then capital of Sikkim, and occupied most of Western Sikkim. They also occupied the entire lower Teesta basin.

The government of Bhutan sent Lam Thinle Druggyal and Zimpon Phurpa as observers. They came up to Munsong Bolgyang situated on the Bhutanese side of the Bhutan-Sikkim border. Bhutan had at first befriended Nepal, for it had wanted Nepal to recognize its title to the Sikkimese territory east of the Teesta River that it had annexed in 1770. It had even received certain estates from Nepal. However, in the 1780s, it realized the danger of Gorkha proximity to its own borders. And, in order to contain Nepal, it started to stay away from the conflicts between Nepal and Sikkim and those between Nepal and Tibet.

The government of Tibet sent Phodang Gawa, Dzongpon of Phari Shar Dzong, to assure help to Sikkim against the Gorkha aggression. It also sent troops from Shekar Dzong under Dapon Kyipuk to drive the Gorkhas out of Sikkim. This compelled the Gorkhas to relinquish part of Western Sikkim. For the help Tibet extended to Sikkim, it took Sikkim's fertile Chhumbi Valley, south of the central ridge of the Himalaya.

Shamarpa Chhodub Gyatsho, the elder brother of the Fourth Panchhen Lama Tenpai Nyima (1781-1852) and the Ninth Gyawa Karmpa of Tibet, had escaped to Kathmandu to seek refuge there. Following the question of asylum to the Shamparpa Lama, the Gorkha army under the command of Kaji Abhiman Singh Basnet,

Kaji Jagjit Pande, Sardar Bam Shah and others attacked Tibet in 1791. For marching into Tibet, they found a pretext, besides differences over currency and other matters, in the Tibetan violation of the traditional Nepalese commercial rights in Tibet. Actually, the Gorkhas had been annoyed by Tibet's intervention in the Nepalese-Sikkimese conflict of 1775 and were looking for an excuse to invade Tibet. When the Gorkhas reached Digarchi/Shigatse, Manchu China, the suzerain of Tibet, intervened. The Manchu expeditionary force marched right up to Nuwakot, the northern gate of the Bagmati Valley, compelling Nepal to accept peace on Manchu terms. Prior to this, Manchu diplomatic efforts to reduce Nepal to the position of a vassal had been in vain.

The Nepal Darbar made land grants to Brahmans for performing mystic rites to ward off the Chinese danger. But the invocation of divine intervention was not helpful. The Gorkhas also sought British help, but the British envoy Captain William Kirkpatrick of the Bengal Army appeared on the scene when the China-Nepal War was already over. The only positive result of the British mission was a treaty of commerce concluded between the East India Company and Nepal at Varanasi on 1 March 1792. This treaty, however, remained a dead letter almost from the day of its conclusion.

The truce, dictated by China through exchange of letters in Nuwakot in September 1792, accorded China the status of suzerain over Nepal. By the agreement of 1792 Nepal undertook to send a mission to Beijing once every five years with presents from the King of Nepal to the Emperor of China. The Gorkhas and the Manchus also agreed to define their boundary fixing it at the 13000 feet high all weather Kuti/Nyalam Pass, the customs line first fixed by Raja Pratap Malla (*r.* 1641-75) as part of a commercial agreement and occupied by Prithvinarayan Shah in 1750. The agreement of 1792 between the Gorkhas and the Manchus could thus be regarded as marking the beginning of the process of boundary-making in the Himalaya.

The Gorkha adventure in Tibet put a stop to the Gorkha expansion in the north and the east. The war with Tibet also compelled the Gorkhas to withdraw from Kumaun, although temporarily.

Ran Bahadur assumed charge as the Maharaja of Nepal in 1795. Ignoring the past, he arraigned his uncle Bahadur Shah and appointed Kaji Damodar Pande as his *Mukhtyar* (Caretaker), the designation of the prime minister of Nepal then.

Ran Bahadur Shah abdicated in favour of his one and a half years old son Girvanayuddha (born of his wife Kantawati, a Maithali Jha Brahman widow, in 1797) bypassing his eldest son Ranoddip (born of Maharani Lalitatripura Sundari Devi of Gulmi) in March 1799. Rajrajeshwari Devi, Chandrawati and Shrividya Devi were his other wives. Bhimsen Thapa had played the role of go-between in the arrangement of Ran Bahadur Shah's marriage with Kantawati. She died two years after the birth of Girvanayuddha (1797-1816). Rani Swarnaprabha, step grand-mother of Girvanayuddha, became his regent. Ran Bahadur Shah retired to Varanasi as an ascetic with the name of Swami Nirgunananda in 1800. Maharani Rajrajeshwari Devi accompanied him to Varanasi. Bhimsen Thapa was the principal aide of Ran Bahadur Shah there. Later, in 1804, Maharani Rajrajeshwari Devi returned to Nepal and became the regent of the infant Maharaja Girvanayuddha Bikram Shah.

Ran Bahadur Shah alias Swamiji Maharaja also returned to Nepal in 1804. Choutariya Sher Bahadur

Shah, the son of the Newar wife of Pratap Singh Shah, and Mukhtyar Damodar Pande went to Thankot to stop him there. The Gorkha army sided with the returning Ran Bahadur Shah and executed Kaji Damodar Pande and his followers. Choutariya Bahadur Shah, Prince Ranoddip and many other kinsmen were also cruelly put to death. Ran Bahadur Shah appointed Bhimsen Thapa as Mukhtyar. Choutariya Sher Bahadur Shah killed Ran Bahadur Shah at the house of Maiju's brother Tribhuvan Khawas (*Hajuria*) on 25 April 1807. Bal Nar Singh Kanwar, the bodyguard of Ran Bahadur Shah, instantly cut down Sher Bahadur Shah. For this deed he received the title of Kaji and the governorship of Palpa. Bal Nar Singh Kanwar was the resident son-in-law of Bhimsen Thapa.

Raja Mahadatt Sen of Palpa had been implicated in the murder of Ran Bahadur Shah. To begin with they appear to have been friendly with each other. Ran Bahadur Shah had even married Mahadatt Sen's daughter.

After the retirement of Ran Bahadur Shah to Varanasi, Mukhtyar Damodar Pande pursued the Gorkha policy of expansion. He contracted a treaty with the British government in Dinapore on 26 October 1801 with the intention to prevent it from supporting Ran Bahadur. He even agreed on an annuity for Ran Bahadur from the revenues of Vijayapur in south-eastern Nepal in order to keep him away at Varanasi. This treaty also provided for the establishment of a British residency in Kathmandu. Later, in 1804, Lord Wellesley, Governor General of the East India Company, abrogated it.

Ran Bahadur Shah is one of Nepal's most fascinating monarchs however the historians may look upon his freakish vignette. There are many interesting anecdotes concerning his royal proclivities. One such anecdote relates to his liking for a certain bull, which he himself allegedly used to feed daily with fresh and dry fruits, bananas, almonds and raisins. The people attending this bull used to call it *sandejyu* ("bull sir"). On its death Ran Bahadur Shah built a *samadhi* (tomb) in its honour. He endowed land for the maintenance of bulls at Deopathan near the Pashupati Temple. From this developed the *goshala* of Nepal.

Mukhtyar Bhimsen Thapa (1775-1839), son of Amar Bahadur Thapa, vigorously pursued the Gorkha policy of expansion. However the treaty between the British government and Maharaja Ranjit Singh of the Panjab (1780-1839), concluded at Amritsar on 12 April 1809, which placed the cis-Satluj states under the protection of the British, frustrated his policy to expand west of the Satluj River. The Gorkha rulers had aimed to bring under their hegemony the entire hill region from Kumaun to Kashmir, where prevailed ethno-cultural customs and beliefs common with those in Nepal. The Gorkhas had crossed the Satluj in 1806.

Bhimsen Thapa organized the Gorkha army into regular platoons and units and constructed cantonments and barracks for the first time. He arranged for the training of the troops and issued blue uniforms for the army. He also started the manufacture of arms and ammunition—guns, pistols, swords, khukris—in the country. He also made several administrative reforms in the country and appointed administrators in civil and revenue posts.

Gorkha encroachments upon the low lands in the British dominions eventually led to a conflict between Nepal and British India. The quarrel centred on the Gorkha claim to certain parts of Purnea, Saran, Gorakhpur and Bareilly districts. There were also disputes over the extradition of dacoits and runaway criminals. On 1 November 1814, in view of the failure of its forces to eject the Gorkhas, the British declared war against Nepal. At first, the British faced several odds. Later, they were successful in their campaigns on the Kumaun, Garhwal and the western Himalaya fronts. On the eve of the war with the Company Nepal's power was at its zenith. Its territories stretched from the Teesta River in the east to the Sutluj River in the west.

The Dhaibung hill, Nuwakot, was the summer residence of the royal house of Nepal up to 1813, a year before the commencement of the Anglo-Nepalese War. Even later it seems to maintain this character It was perhaps to maintain the tradition of his predecessors that Maharajadhiraj Prithvi Bir Bikram Shah Dev (*r.* 1881-1911) set up his summer camp there.

The treaty of peace, dictated by the British and signed at Segowley/Sugauli (district Motihari, North Bihar) on 2 December 1815 and ratified at Calcutta on 4 March 1816, fixed the Kali River as the western limit of Nepal and the Mechi River as its eastern limit. Nepal ceded to the British all the lands the British had claimed prior to 1 November 1814. It also ceded Kumaun and Garhwal as well as the hill domains further west to the British. The British transferred the extensive tract east of the Mechi River to the Sikkimpati. The treaty of 1815 accepted the right of the British government to arbitrate in disputes between Nepal and Sikkim. The King of Nepal also engaged never to take or retain in his service any British subject, nor the subject of any European or American state, without the consent of the British government.

To obtain access to the wool-producing districts of Western Tibet and secure the routes that led to them, the British government retained the territory between the Kali and Satluj rivers. To ensure for itself the use of routes to Tibet passing through the Arun and Karnali valleys respectively, the British government also considered setting up the territories immediately east and west of the Arun and Karnali rivers as separate political entities under the Nepalis subservient to it. Perhaps the British themselves did not want to be in Nepal. However, on 8 December 1816, the British government returned to Nepal for various considerations part of the territory that had been ceded to it.

The Anglo-Nepalese treaty of 1815 was quite different from the Anglo-Nepalese treaties of 1792 and 1801. It established the principle of perpetual peace and friendship between British India and Nepal but it placed no restrictions on the right of Nepal to maintain diplomatic relations with foreign states. Nepal continued to maintain its diplomatic relations with Tibet, China and Bhutan. As such, this treaty constituted recognition of Nepal as a sovereign state.

The British government stationed a resident in Kathmandu. The British resident gradually arrogated to himself the same rights as the British residents that the British government had stationed in those princely states in India which had accepted British paramountcy. The residency in Nepal also served as an observation post on Chinese activity in Tibet and beyond. The Manchu rulers of China had no serious objection to the stationing of a British resident in Nepal. The Gorkhas, of course, tried to get rid of the British resident by pretending that China did not want him there.

Although the British defeated the Gorkhas they were not able to establish their suzerainty over Nepal as the Manchus did in 1792. Although they eventually succeeded in preventing the Gorkhas from having any political relations with the princely states in India and even treating Nepal as a native state up to a time, they were not able to abolish the Manchu suzerainty over Nepal up to the fall of the Manchu Ch'ing dynasty of China. The British resident really was a diplomatic envoy to the Nepal Darbar, the court of Nepal.

Bhimsen Thapa found it hard to reconcile himself to the humiliation implied in the treaty of 1815. He, therefore, tried to set up other powers against the British. The death in 1832 of Dowager Maharani Tripura Sundari Devi, who had been regent of Yuvaraj Rajendra (1816-47) since 1816, weakened Bhimsen Thapa's position. Yuvaraj Rajendra attained majority and assumed charge as Maharaja of Nepal in 1833. He arraigned Bhimsen Thapa on 18 May 1839 and sent him in chains to Boomkot, northwest of Kathmandu. According to the Pandes and other rivals, Bhimsen Thapa had usurped royal powers. The Pandes had re-emerged as a powerful faction after the mid-1830s as a result of the patronage of Maharaja Rajendra's first wife Maharani Samrajya-lakshmi Devi and the eclipse of the Thapas from the Nepalese political scene.

The Maharani took active part in state politics much against the wishes of her husband. She wanted him to abdicate in favour of her son. She found Ranjang Pande, son of Damodar Pande, a ready tool for the fulfilment of her objective. She sent Choutariya Pushkar Shah to Beijing much against Bhimsen Thapa's wish in July 1837. On return from Beijing in September 1838, Pushkar Shah shared power with Ranjang Pande.

Bhimsen Thapa committed suicide in prison on 29 July 1839. A *lal mohar*, a red seal royal decree, deprived the Bagale clan of Bhimsen Thapa from receiving any assignment for seven generations. The Nepal Darbar banished Bhimsen Thapa's family to a prison in the remote western hills. What a tragic end to a great precursor of the later Rana ministers of Nepal.

Raghunath Pande, the leader of one (Brahman) of the many court factions, replaced Bhimsen Thapa. As the leader of the coalition ministry, he avoided getting involved in the harem politics. However, he was unable to control the warring factions. On his resignation in September 1839, Ranjang Pande became Mukhtyar in early December 1839.

Ranjang Pande concerted with other powers against the British, who could not object to the Nepal Darbar's establishing contact with other powers as there was nothing in the Anglo-Nepalese treaty of 1815 forbidding Nepal from doing so. But, following negotiations, the Nepal Darbar agreed on 6 November 1839, to give up its right to have intercourse with the princely states of India beyond the Ganga without the consent of the British government. This was a real setback, although temporary, for Nepal's manoeuvres to enlist the support of the Marathas, the Rajputs and the Sikhs in India and of Afghanistan, Burma and China then seeking the opportunity of lining themselves up against British expansionism and continued to do so until the overthrow of Ranjang Pande on 1 November 1840 and the death of Maharani Samrajyalakshmi Devi on 6 October 1842 enroute to Varanasi.

The appointment of Choutariya Fatehjang Shah as Mukhtyar marked the end of the anti-British period in the history of modern Nepal. The years 1823-1843 were really the most critical years for the British in Nepal. Nepal, along with Afghanistan and Burma, presented a danger of war to the British in 1839. The British resident B.H. Hodgson had even to clap Maharaja Rajendra into confinement at the desire of Lord Ellenborough, the most autocratic Governor General of British India from 1838 to 1842.

Maharani Rajyalakshmi Devi, the second wife of Maharaja Rajendra and sister of Maharani Samrajyalakshmi Devi, does not seem to have received her conjugal and political rights consequent on the death of Samrajyalakshmi Devi even though he betook himself to, and abode in her apartments.

Mathbar Singh Thapa, a nephew of Bhimsen Thapa who was then living in exile in British India, returned to Kathmandu on 17 April 1843. The Nepal Darbar restored the family of Mathbar Singh Thapa to the enjoyment of all civil and religious privileges in the country. Choutariya Ranodatt Shah and others also returned from India to Nepal.

Mathbar Singh Thapa succeeded Fatehjang Shah as Mukhtyar and Commander-in-Chief on 25 December 1843. There was much palace intrigue during his time. An assassin shot Mathbar Singh in the Hanuman Dhoka palace on 18 May 1845. His eldest son Ranojjval Singh escaped to India along with his associates. Fatehjang Shah became Mukhtyar in the care-taker council of ministers. The chaos that had been witnessed since 1833 culminated in the Kot palace massacre—a gruesome event in which a large number of influential Nepalese elites, including Fatehjang Shah and his son Khadgavikram Shah, were killed in an hour on the midnight of 15 September 1846.

Jang Bahadur Kanwar (1816-77), a favourite of Yuvaraj Surendra and the eldest son of Bal Nar Singh Kanwr from his second wife and a nephew of Mathbar Singh Thapa and the Commander-in-Chief of Nepal, played a historic part in the Kot massacre. With the elimination of all those capable of challenging him, Jang Bahadur became Mukhtyar on 16 September.

On 23 November 1846 Maharaja Rajendra, his second wife Rajyalakshmi Devi and their followers left for Varanasi. When he returned to Nepal on 12 May 1847, the authorities apprehended him, dethroned him and shut him up in the Bhadgau fortress. There he died miserably.

The authorities also deprived Rani Rajyalakshmi Devi of her position and power and expelled her to Varanasi. She had desired either of her sons Princes Ratendra and Birendra to become the Maharaja. Within 25 years she was without progeny and dynasty.

Yuvaraj Surendra (1829-81) became Maharaja with the help of Jang Bahadur Kanwar and his associates. He appointed Jang Bahadur as Mukhtyar the same year. Maharaja Surendra authorized Jang Bahadur Kanwar and his seven brothers to suffix *Rana* to their names.

Up to the time of Maharaja Surendra Bir Bikram Shah Dev the royal house reigned from the Hanuman Dhoka Darbar even though Prithvinarayan Shah had built the Kailash Darbar. The Narayanahiti Darbar, the present royal palace, is from the time of Maharajadhiraj Prithvi Bir Bikram Shah Dev.

CHAPTER 4

Nepal 1846–1951

MAHARAJA Surendra, who had lived through the tumultuous period of intrigues and plots, took to comfort and ease. This enabled Jang Bahadur to strengthen his position. Now, except his own supporter Prince Upendra, he had to heed none else. He eliminated members of the Basnet and Pande families, who had served Prithvinarayan Shah and his successors in various capacities to build modern Nepal, from high offices of state traditionally conferred upon them. Within two years of his becoming Mukhtyar, he appointed his seven brothers and nephews to all high offices vacant since the Kot and Bhandkhal massacres. Bam Bahadur became commander-in-chief and deputy prime minister, Badri Nar Singh army chief, Krishna Bahadur chief of administration, Jagat Shamsher and Dhir Shamsher captain and so on.

Two years after the enthronement of Maharaja Surendra Bir Bikram Shah Dev, that is, in 1849, began the Second Anglo-Sikh War. Jang Bahadur expressed his readiness to help the British, who declined his offer of help. After the war, he allowed Rani Chand Kaur, the wife of Maharaja Kharak Singh of the Panjab, to seek asylum in Nepal.

Having consolidated his position and power, Jang Bahadur crossed the seas to go to England and Europe in the summer of 1850. He did so despite the prohibitory injunction of the Nepalese Hindu custom. His entourage consisted of forty high dignitaries including Jagat Shamsher and Dhir Shamsher. The British accorded him a great welcome and honour. He reached an understanding with the British to apprehend in India the Nepalese opponents of the Rana rule in Nepal. The British upheld this understanding until their departure from India in the summer of 1947. Anyway the visit of Jang Bahadur to England was the first official contact of the Nepal Darbar with the Court of St. James.

Within only a few days of his return from abroad, Jang Bahadur managed to dispense without the support of Prince Upendra.

Jang Bahadur codified in 1854 the laws of Nepal, the *Mulki Ain* of Maharaja Surendra, which included, among religious and social usages: "The Shastras as well as the laws permit men of the four *varnas* and the thirty-six *jats* to marry their younger and elder sisters-in-law." Perhaps he did this in view of the forthcoming conflict with Tibet, which he was then contemplating and which might produce any number of war widows.

Jang Bahadur attacked Tibet in the summer of 1855, ostensibly to punish the Tibetans for their alleged misbehaviour towards the Nepalese traders in Tibet. General Dhir Shamsher led the attack. Perhaps China's inability to come to the help of Tibet had prompted Jang Bahadur to invade Tibet. For even as the Opium War (1840-42) had prevented China from helping Tibet against the invasion of the Dogras of Jammu during 1841-42, the Taiping Rebellion (1850-64) had prevented China to come to the rescue of Tibet against the Nepalese invasion. After a short period of hostilities and protracted negotiations, the Nepalis and the Tibetans signed a treaty of peace in Kathmandu on 24 March 1856. Interestingly, both sides acknowledged, in the preamble of the treaty, the suzerainty of China. This reflected the Rana rulers' effort for an equation in their relations with the British and the Chinese. At the same time they could say that they did so in consonance with the Chinese-Nepalese agreement of 1792. The Manchu *Amban* (Minister) in Tibet, being satisfied that Nepal pledged to continue to pay respect to the Manchu emperor in spite of this war put his seal of approval on the treaty between Nepal and Tibet.

Nepal bound itself to give "all assistance that may be in its power to the government of Tibet, if the troops of any other king invade that country". Nepal gained several political and commercial concessions, including extra-territorial rights in Tibet. The government of Tibet ceded to Nepal certain areas of the frontier district of Kerung/Kyirong. Tibet also bound itself to pay to Nepal Rs 10,000 annually. Nepal continued to enjoy these rights and privileges for a hundred years, precisely until 20 September 1956, when under the Chinese Nepalese Agreement, it accepted the principle of China's sovereignty over Tibet.

Jang Bahadur built the frontier fortress of Rasuwa Garhi in the trans-Himalaya territory of Tibet during the Nepalese-Tibetan War of 1855-56.

Jang Bahadur had not succeeded in persuading Bhutan to side with Nepal in the war against Tibet. After 1856, relations between Nepal and Bhutan, which had always been most friendly, became merely formal. These relations ended altogether as the consequence of the Anglo-Bhutanese treaty of 8 January 1910, which placed Bhutan's external relations under the control of the British government in India.

Jang Bahadur resigned on 1 August 1856 and installed his younger brother General Bam Bahadur in his place. General Bam Bahadur was already the commander-in-chief and deputy prime minister of Nepal. Jang

Bahadur did so in order to please his brothers and other dignitaries. But, on 6 August 1856, he obtained from Maharaja Surendra the absolute right to the office of prime minister of Nepal with the title of *Maharaja*. Maharaja Surendra himself took the title of *Maharajadhiraj*, colloquially *Adhiraj*. The absolute right of Prime Minister and the title *Maharaja* were made hereditary in Jang Bahadur's family. Consequently the titles Maharajadhiraj and Maharaja came popularly to be known as Shri 5 (Five) and Shri 3 (Three) according to the number of Shris in the address of the Maharajadhiraj and the Maharaja. The title of Maharaja ended with the ending of the Rana primacy in the politics of Nepal and the appellation of Shri 3 along with it in the early 1950s. The Nepalis, however, continue to refer to their Maharajadhiraj by the appellation *Shri 5* and the Government of Nepal as *Shri 5 ko Sarkar*.

Before the conquest of the Malla kingdoms of the Bagmati Valley in 1768-69, Prithvinarayan Shah like his predecessors prefixed only one shri to his name. After the conquest, he prefixed two shris to his name presumably to conform to the practice of the Malla kings who had two shris as prefixes to their names. Later, three shris preceded his name and the name of his successors on the throne of Nepal.

The coup of Jang Bahadur overthrew absolute monarchy in Nepal and established autocratic oligarchy instead. The overthrow of absolute monarchy, however, was by coup, and not by revolution. Hence there was no abolition of feudalism in the country.

Jang Bahadur combined in himself the two high offices of the Prime Minister and the Supreme Commander-in-chief, his second or nearest brother being Mukhtyar and Commander-in-Chief or Chief Sahebjyu of the Nepalese army directly under him. He willed, prompted no doubt by a sense of the probable consequences, that his brothers should share his work. He also set up the roll of succession to the office of prime minister among his brothers in order of seniority of age and thence among his sons in the same order.

Jang Bahadur continued in office till his death on 25 February 1877 except for the interval from 1 August 1856 to 25 May 1857. His second term as the Maharaja and Prime Minister of Nepal started on the death of Bam Bahadur on 24 May 1857. Bam Bahadur was the first prime minister in the history of modern Nepal to die in office peacefully.

The British found a trusted friend in Jang Bahadur. Jang Bahadur offered military aid to the British during the rebellion of 1857-58. The British accepted the Nepalese troops as auxiliaries to the British army commanded by Sir Colin Campbell on 18 November 1857. Jang Bahadur personally marched with the Nepalese contingent to help the British in suppressing the revolt in Awadh. His attitude towards the Anglo-Sikkimese complications of 1860-61 and the Anglo-Bhutanese War of 1864-65 is not so clear.

Jang Bahadur also tried to go with the resurgent tide in India and granted political asylum in Nepal to certain political personages from India. However, it appears, he did not treat them well. For instance, although he had allowed Rani Jindan Kalan, the youngest wife of Maharaja Ranjit Singh and the mother of Maharaja Dalip Singh, to settle near his own house at Thapathali, he imposed humiliating indignities and restrictions on her under the pressure of the British Residency. Of course the British did not seriously ask for her extradition. Maharaja Dalip Singh took her to England, where she died in 1863. She was commonly known as Rani Jindan.

For his personal services, the British rewarded Jang Bahadur suitably and conferred titles of G.C.B. and K.C.S.I. on him. By a treaty signed in Kathmandu on 1 November 1860, the British government of India also restored to Nepal the entire Western Tarai between the rivers Kali and Rapti in appreciation of Jang Bahadur's helping the British quell the rebellion in India in 1857. The Nepalis still call the territories *Naya Muluk* (New Dominion). This territory, the present districts of Banke Bardiya and Kailali Kanchanpur—ever since Nepal's principal districts—had belonged to Awadh. Nepal had annexed this territory during 1800-14. The Nepal Darbar had ceded it to the British government after the Anglo-Nepalese War of 1814-15. The British eventually became the protectors of the Ranas. They never cared as to what happened inside Nepal or ignored the happenings there. They allowed the Ranas a free hand in the management of the affairs of the country. The arrangement continued until the British withdrawal from India in 1947.

Jang Bahadur also maintained his relations with the Manchus of China. The Manchu emperor conferred a title of honour on the King of Nepal. The Manchu emperor also conferred on Jang Bahadur the title *Thong-lin Bing-ko Kang-wang Syan*, the highest rank in the Manchu army, in 1871. Subsequently this became the Manchu practice of conferring titles of honour on the king and prime minister of Nepal.

Ranoddip Singh, a younger brother of Jang Bahadur and next in line according to the roll of succession set up by him, succeeded Jang Bahadur on his death on 25 February 1877 as the Maharaja and Prime Minister of Nepal and so on. He proved to be the only exception to do so. The Rana prime ministers who succeeded Ranoddip Singh did not strictly follow the roll of succession set up by Jang Bahadur. According to the roll of succession, Ranoddip Singh appointed his younger brother Jagat Shamsher as the commander-in-chief of the Nepalese army.

In January 1878 a Manchu officer visited Kathmandu to congratulate Ranoddip Singh on his succession as the Maharaja and Prime Minister of Nepal, and to confer a title of honour upon him. Tibet considered this tactics of China as appeasement of Nepal, its enemy of the Nepal-Tibet War of 1855-56.

Ranoddip Singh declared his intention to maintain the status quo of Jang Bahadur's policy of friendly co-operation with the British. Despite this Nepal's relations with the British deteriorated. This was mainly due to his younger brother Dhir Shamsher as the Commander-in-Chief after the death of General Jagat Samsher in 1879. General Dhir Shamsher controlled the real power in Nepal until his death in October 1884. Essentially a militarist, he steadily tried to increase the strength of the Nepalese army. Despite the fact that he was the same man who was with the Nepalese troops to support the British army in 1857, British officials considered him to be anti-British and did not want him to equip the Nepalese army with arms of precision. The Government of India did not give the Nepal Darbar permision to purchase arms and munitions on the excuse that Nepal might go to war with Tibet. No doubt there was serious tension between Nepal and Tibet in 1882-84.

Yuvaraj Prithvi (1875-1911) became the Maharajadhiraj of Nepal on 11 December 1881. His father Yuvaraj Trailokya (1847-77) had died before succeeding his father Maharajadhiraj Surendra. Jang Bahadur had married his three daughters with Yuvaraj Trailokya in 1858. Yuvaraja Trailokya tried hard to restore the Nepalese monarchy to its pre-1846 position. This greatly angered the ruling Ranas especially Dhir Shamsher.

A conspiracy by Bir Shamber, Dambar Shamsher, Khadga Shamsher, Chandra Shamsher and Bhim Shamsher, all sons of Dhir Shamsher from different wives, led to the assassination of Maharaja Ranoddip Singh and many others, who might succeed him, on the night of 22 November 1885. Dambar Shamsher had fired the first shot. Bir Shamsher was then away in India attending the darbar of Lord Duferin, Viceroy of India from 1884 to 1888. He became Maharaja and Prime Minister in 1886. He declared the roll of succession among his brothers, but included his own sons Chakra Shamsher, Rudra Shamsher, Tej Shamsher and Pratap Shamsher. Ranoddip Singh had no issues. Khadga Shamsher became the Commander-in-Chief, and so on. He died in exile in Varanasi on 22 December 1901.

Maharajadhiraj Prithvi Bir Bikram Shah Dev (*r.* 1881-1911) was a mere spectator in this high drama for power in Nepal. He was a mere child of 9 years then. One can imagine his pain and confusion under the circumstances of the time. He had just given expression to his kind feeling towards Maharaja Ranoddip Singh and his wife Maharani Haripriya. After the attempted assassination of Maharaja Ranoddip Singh in the summer of 1883, he had conveyed deep appreciation of the services of Maharani Haripriya in looking after him while he was yet Yuvaraj.

Relations between the British government of India and the Nepal Darbar remained one of mutual distrust. During the Anglo-Tibetain clash over Sikkim in the summer of 1888, Maharaja Bir Shamsher wrote to the ministers of the *Kashag*/Council of Tibet not to misunderstand British intentions. British officials looked even upon this manifestation of friendship by Bir Shamsher as sham. But the handing over by the Nepal Darbar to the British government of Maharaja Thutob Namgyal (*r.* 1868-1914) of Sikkim whom it had captured while he was trying to escape to Tibet through Nepal led eventually to the improvement of relations between the British and Nepal. The British government conferred on Maharaja Bir Samsher the title of KCSI as a mark of appreciation of service thus rendered. Really friendly relations between them, however, developed only with the coming to power of Chandra Shamsher in the summer of 1901. Maharaja Bir Shamsher had most uneasy relations with Lord Curzon, who became Viceroy and Governor General of India in 1899. Curzon tried to deal directly with the Maharajadhiraj of Nepal like the heads of the princely states in India.

Dev Shamsher, who succeeded Bir Shamsher on his death on 5 March 1901, was Maharaja and Prime Minister only for three months (5 March—26 June 1901). For the sake of administrative consultation, he started the practice of daily morning collective salute to the Maharajadhiraj. He established the first *Gorkhapatra* weekly, under the independent editorship of Madan Dev Sharma, for the purpose of the news of the world. He also thought of abolishing slavery from the country. All this alarmed the Ranas. The spread of education in the country, feared the Ranas, might imbue the people with ideas of popular government. The Ranas looked upon Dev Shamsher's reforms as harmful to Rana interests, ousted him and banished him to Dhankuta in East Nepal. Dev Shamsher eventually escaped to India and lived in Mussoorie till his death on 20 February 1914. Again, as in 1881, Maharajadhiraj Prithvi was a helpless spectator in this high drama for power in his kingdom.

Chandra Shamsher succeeded Dev Shamsher as the Maharaja and Prime Minister on 25 June 1901 in a bloodless *coup*. Under Bir Shamsher, Chandra Shamsher was third in line of succession to the office of prime minister. With Chandra Shamsher succeeding Dev Shamsher, succession to the office of the Maharaja and Prime Minister of Nepal became more or less an orderly affair.

Chandra Shamsher established the first Ayurved school in the country in 1915. He realized the value of the traditional system of Ayurvedic medicine after he himself had suffered from tuberculosis and Ayurvedic medicine was the only medicine then available for its treatment. He also created an endowment to finance a sanitorium. He created the Gorkha Bhasha Pracharini Samiti, later renamed Nepali Bhasha Prakashani Samiti. He also established the first English medium college in the country, naming it the Tri-Chandra College after Maharajadhiraj Tribhuvan Bir Bikram Shah Dev (1906-55) and himself in 1918. He issued khaki uniforms and khaki military hats for the soldiers of the Nepalese army. He cancelled the rule of land grants to the Nepalese army officers and soldiers instead of salaries.

Maharaja Chandra Shamsher obtained the formal consent of Maharajadhiraj Prithvi to assume, in advance, all public acts of his prime minister as having the full royal approval. He also put the scions of the Rana family into A, B and C categories and changed the roll of succession by entitling only "A" class Ranas to the office of the Maharaja and Prime Minister of the country.

Aware of the tiff between Lord Curzon and Maharaja Bir Shamsher, Maharaja Chandra Shamsher thus stated his intention to be cooperative with the Government of India in a letter to Lord Curzon:

> I shall take this opportunity of assuring your Excellency's Government that I shall always deem it a sacred duty and valued privilege, not only to culti-

> vate and continue unimpaired the friendly relations subsisting between the governments of India and Nepal, but to strengthen and improve them, so that we may realize all those expectations which the association with such a power like that of England naturally raises in our mind. I am fully conscious that our interests can best be served by the continuance of friendly relations between India and Nepal.

The Ranas scrupulously maintained this policy of friendship with the British until the latter's withdrawal from India.

From the time of Jang Bahadur to the time of the British departure from India, except for the brief interval of 1885-1901, Nepal's relations with the British remained mostly cordial. Despite the Nepalese-Tibetan treaty of Kathmandu of 1856, which bound Nepal to come to the assistance of Tibet in the event of any foreign invasion, Nepal helped the British government during its military expedition to Tibet in 1903-04. It supported the British government because the ascendancy of any other power in Tibet would have endangered the trade and other interests of Nepal in Tibet. Curzon accepted the offer of yaks by Chandra Shamsher only to impress the government of Tibet that Nepal was on the Brtish side. He felt that although the alliance with Nepal might not strengthen the British military force to Tibet, but the appearance of one might help to impress. However, after 1904, the British never allowed Nepal, in the British interest, to interfere in Tibet. Nepal strongly resented it but it could do nothing concerning the British attitude in the matter.

Nepal also helped the British during the First World War (1914-18) and the Third Anglo-Afghan War (1919).

Chandra Shamsher sent Padma and Babbar to Wazirstan on 27 December 1919. For this help the British sanctioned an annual subsidy of Rs 10,00,000 to Nepal, later made a part of the annual subsidy vide the treaty of 21 December 1923.

Several recommendations in 1919-1920 led the British government to change the designation of its representative at Kathmandu from British resident to envoy at the court of Nepal and the name of the residency to legation. It called the Maharajadhiraj of Nepal His Majesty the King of Nepal. The title Nepal Darbar became the Government of Nepal. It did so to emphasize that Nepal was different from the princely states in India in view of Nepal's sensitivity to any impugnment of its independent status.

The British government of India and the Rana government of Nepal concluded a treaty of perpetual peace and friendship signed by Frederick O'Connor and Chandra Shamsher in Kathmandu on 21 December 1923. The treaty of 1923 confirmed all treaties and agreements between India and Nepal since the treaty of 1815 except as far as they had been altered by it. It replaced the treaty of 1815. It also cancelled the engagement of 1839 prohibiting Nepal from establishing links with the princely states in India. It also gave the government of Nepal the right to employ or retain any person. Above all, it recognized Nepal's right to procure arms and ammunition from or through India.

All this did not, however, amount to the recognition of Nepal as a fully sovereign state. The British allowed the Nepalese legation in London, first established in the early 1930s, to deal with the British Foreign Office only through the India Office. This reflected the actual political status of Nepal up to the British withdrawal from India even though the Government of India Act of 1935 did not consider Nepal to be within its purview. The Ranas always feared that the British might reduce Nepal to the status of a princely state of India.

The Rana period cannot be considered to be a bright period in the history of modern Nepal. The Ranas used their absolute authority only to perpetuate their own position and power in the country. The first Rana prime minister, Jang Bahadur Rana, seemed to have aimed at achieving sovereign position in Nepal but failed in that design. He had, however, succeeded in achieving *de facto* sovereignty over Nepal. His successors had inherited this position. The Rana Prime Ministers Bir Shamsher (1885-1901), Chandra Shamsher (1901-29) and Juddha Shamsher (1933-45) were the paragons of the system of polity created by Jang Bahadur. The Rana polity grew up to the end of the prime ministership of Maharaja Bir Shamsher. Maharaja Juddha Shamsher of the second generation of the Rana regime separated the judiciary from the executive. Up to his time, the civil authorities had exercised both the administrative and judicial powers in the country. The Rana regime lasted over a century from 1846 to 1951 and the Rana polity remained unchanged until its very end.

CHAPTER 5

Nepal 1951-

RANA autocracy did not long remain unchallenged. There were several plots, devised mostly by discontented nobles and high dignitaries belonging to non-Rana families even though they did not succeed to overthrow the Rana regime. Owing to the impact made by the spread of education in the Bagmati Valley in the first part of the twentieth century, public feeling too turned against Rana despotism. There arose in the 1930s many socio-cultural and socio-religious organizations in the country, like the Praja Parishad (1936), indicating popular disaffection with the Rana regime.

The Rana rulers greatly feared the impact on Nepal of the freedom movement in India. They developed a policy of aloofness from the struggle in India and spared no effort to suppress the organizations and the individuals in the country connected with them or behind them. They even charged Maharajadhiraj Tribhuvan (*r.* 1911-55) with complicity in a plot by Shukra Raj Joshi, Gagan Lal Shrestha, Dashrath Chand and Dharma Bhakta Mathema against Maharaja Juddha Shamsher in 1939-40. Dharma Bhakta, King Tribhuvan's physical instructor, secretly obtained for him books of civics and politics from India. Shukra Raj and Dharma Bhakta were done to death by hanging near Pashupati on 26 January 1941. Gagan Lal and Dashrath Chand were shot dead. Juddha Shamsher also attempted to dethrone Tribhuvan in 1940.

Strong opposition against the Rana rule developed in the country in the 1940s. The Nepalese youths, who had either participated in the freedom movement in India or witnessed the "Quit India" Movement in the summer of 1942, started political parties like the All India Nepali Congress (Varanasi, 1946), the Nepali Rashtriya Congress (Calcutta, 1947) and the Nepali Loktantrik Dal (Calcutta, 1948). The Nepali Rashtriya Congress/Nepali National Congress launched an agitation in the Eastern Tarai in the spring of 1947. This agitation also spread to the other parts of the Tarai, and ultimately to the Bagmati Valley itself. The Nepali Loktantrik Dal/Nepali Democratic Party consisted of prominent members of the "C" Class Ranas who had been deprived of the enjoyment of position and power in the system on the basis of high and low castes like Mahabir Shamsher and Subarna Shamsher and had at its disposal all their material resources. Later, on 8 April 1950, it merged with the Nepali Rashtriya Congress to form the Nepali Congress.

Theoretically the King of Nepal was the source and fountain of all authority in the country, but, practically he was the virtual prisoner of his Rana prime minister. The Rana prime minister was *the* political power in the country then. The prime minister had reduced the king to the status of a political non-entity. In the political change of 1951, King Tribhuvan, who was in search of opportunities to enable him to restore the power and authority of the monarchy, supported the Nepali Congress. "C" class Ranas supported both the King and the Nepali Congress against the Rana regime.

The Ranas were not able to resist the demand for democratic form of government in the country. Maharaja Padma Shamsher of the third generation of the Rana regime, Prime Minister since 29 November 1945 promulgated the Nepal Government Act of 1947 to be effective from 1 April 1948. The Act of 1947 had been drafted in consultation with eminent jurists from India—Sri Prakasa of Varanasi, personal representatives of Jawaharlal Nehru, and Ram Ugra Singh of the University of Delhi.

The Act of 1947 had envisaged election to three Panchayat bodies at the village, district and national levels. It had restricted adult franchise to the village Panchayat; it had restricted voting rights to the district Panchayat to members of the village Panchayat, etc. It had envisaged two houses of the national legislature (the *Bharadari Sabha*: Upper House and the *Rashtra Sabha*: Lower House). It had envisaged equal powers for the two houses. The Prime Minister had reserved to himself the final say of legislation. He had also reserved to himself the power to act in a situation of emergency. And so on and so forth.

The Ranas were unhappy with the Act of 1947 because it was much too radical. They depreciated Maharaja Padma's liberalist outlook. The people were unhappy because it kept intact the rights and privileges of the Ranas. They intensified the agitation in the Bagmati Valley for civil rights. Under the force of circumstances, Padma Shamsher resigned his office of prime minister on 30 April 1948 and settled down at Ranchi (Bihar) in India. Mohan Shamsher, the leader of militant Ranas, became the Maharaja and Prime Minister of Nepal.

Independent India inherited the British treaty position in Nepal. Nepal wanted to establish relations with national India on the same basis as that with British India. Nepal and India first concluded a "standstill agreement". They signed a treaty of perpetual peace and friendship in Kathmandu on 31 July 1950.

The treaty of 1950 provided for cooperation and

consultation between India and Nepal in matters of common concern to them such as defence and security. It also provided for the government of Nepal freely to import, from or through India into Nepal, arms and ammunition or warlike material and equipment necessary for the security of Nepal. Among other things, it also provided, on a reciprocal basis, free movement to the nationals of one country in the territories of the other. Briefly, the 1950 treaty established special relations between India and Nepal.

Certain anti-Rana politicians like Tanka Prasad Acharya of the Praja Parishad, then in gaol were particularly critical of the provision in the treaty of special relations between Nepal and India. According to them, this provision circumscribed Nepal's sovereignty. But Tanka Prasad Acharya, when he himself was the Premier of Nepal from 1956 to 1957, rejected the view that the Indo-Nepalese treaty of 1950 put limits on Nepal's freedom of action in any way.

The Nepali Congress decided, in September 1950, to launch an agitation for the establishment of a democratic government in Nepal. Maharaja Mohan Shamsher dubbed the Nepali Congress as an anti-national party. He accused it of trying to subvert Nepal's independence with India's help. Several prominent leaders of the Nepali Congress had taken part in the national struggle in India. The Government of India advised Maharaja Mohan Shamsher to keep pace with the rapidly changing world. Mohan Shamsher resented the advice and accused India of trying to influence, and interfere in the affairs of Nepal.

In September 1950 Maharaja Mohan Shamsher sent up to Maharajadhiraj Tribhuvan for approval an order sentencing certain persons for allegedly conspiring against his life. The Maharajadhiraj, for the first time after the rise of Jang Bahadur, refused to give his assent. Consequently the Maharaja placed additional restrictions on the movements of the Maharajadhiraj. On 6 November, Maharajadhiraj Tribhuvan, accompanied by Yuvaraj Mahendra (b. 1920) and other members of the royal family except the three-year old Prince Gyanendra, a younger son of Yuvaraj Mahendra and a grandson of Maharajadhiraj Tribhuvan, escaped to the Indian embassy in Kathmandu. On 7 November Maharaja Mohan Shamsher announced the deposition of Maharajadhiraj Tribhuvan and Yuvaraj Mahendra and other members of the royal family accompanying them and installed Prince Gyanendra as the Maharajadhiraj of Nepal. On 11 November, an armed insurrection started by the Nepali Congress followed this dramatic, momentous event in the country.

On 6 December, Prime Minister Jawaharlal Nehru stated in the *Sansad*/Parliament that India recognized only Maharajadhiraj Tribhuvan as the head of state of Nepal. He further stated:

> Frankly, we do not like and shall not brook any foreign interference in Nepal. We recognize Nepal as an independent country and wish her well. But even a child knows that one cannot go to Nepal without passing through India. Therefore, no other country can have as intimate a relationship with Nepal as ours is. We would like every other country to appreciate the intimate geographical and cultural relationship that exists between India and Nepal . . . . Our interest in the internal conditions of Nepal has become still more acute and personal, because of the developments across our borders, especially in China and Tibet. Besides our sympathetic interest in Nepal, we are also interested in the security of

> our country. From time immemorial, the Himalayas have provided us with a magnificent frontier. Of course, they are no longer as impassable as they used to be but they are still fairly effective. We cannot allow that barrier to be penetrated, because it is also the principal barrier to India. Therefore, much as we appreciate the independence of Nepal, we cannot allow anything to go wrong in Nepal or permit the barrier to be crossed or weakened, because that would be a risk to our own security . . . .

As a consequence, it appears, no country, which had recognized Nepal after the Second World War, recognized the installation of the infant king. Kathmandu and Washington had established diplomatic relations in April 1947 for the first time. Perhaps the geographical circumstance of Nepal's location or India's position in Nepal under the treaty of 31 July 1950 stayed their hand. The People's Republic of China and Nepal did not yet recognize each other. It is, however, not very difficult to visualize the attitude of China in the matter in the light of the nature of relations between China and Nepal in recent years.

On 8 December, the Government of India sent a memorandum to the Government of Nepal which said that its primary objective was only to strengthen the independence of Nepal and to enable it to make progress and grow strong. It also suggested that the Government of Nepal should adopt such constitutional changes as would satisfy popular opinion and non-official Nepalese organizations. The changes suggested included the setting up of an interim government under a Rana prime minister, with equal representation of both Rana and popular interests and with joint responsibility. They also provided for the continuance of Maharajadhiraj Tribhuvan as the head of state of Nepal.

Having regard to the circumstances then obtaining, the Ranas had no alternative other than acceptance of the proposals of the Government of India. Several important areas in East, South and West Nepal were aflame with revolt then. The *Mukti Sena* (Liberation Army) had seized many district headquarters. On 10 January 1951 Tribhuvan appealed to the Mukti Sena to lay down its arms in the interests of the country. Leaders of the Nepali Congress at first ignored the appeal. After discussions with the Government of India on 16 January, however, they announced cease-fire and appealed to the people to help restore law and order in the country.

On 12 February, Maharajadhiraj Tribhuvan and the Rana government accepted the proposals of the Government of India. The accord negotiated with the mediation of the Government of India restored paramountcy to the Crown. Later, this accord came to be known as the Delhi Settlement of 1951. On 15 February, Maharajadhiraj Tribhuvan and members of the royal family returned to Kathmandu to the cheerful and enthusiastic welcome of the people amid scenes of jubilation and rejoicing. On 18 February, Mohan Shamsher, the last Rana prime minister, became the first prime minister of the coalition government. Thus ended the Rana period in the history of modern Nepal.

Maharajadhiraj Tribhuvan set up the interim government of Nepal under the *Antarim Shashan Vidhan* (Interim Administration Constitution) promulgated by him on 10 April 1951. The people, in consequence, felt emancipated in spirit and thought.

On 16 June, in order to spell away fears of India's interference in Nepal, Prime Minister Nehru said in a public address in Kathmandu:

> If you seek our help in, say, technical or other spheres, we will do our utmost to be useful to you, but we never want to interfere . . . .

The Rana-Nepali Congress coalition collapsed eventually. Mohan Shamsher and the Rana group resigned on 12 November. Maharajadhiraj Tribhuvan accepted their resignations and dissolved the coalition government. He invited M.P. Koirala to form the first non-Rana government on 15 November. Owing to the unsatisfactory performance of the (M.P.) Koirala government, he dissolved it after nine months. After ruling directly for a while, he experimented with other party governments until his passing away in Zurich on 13 March 1955.

The Ranas turned anti-India and anti-Nepali Congress and transferred their loyalties to the Royal Palace. They set up their own political party—the Gorkha Dal, later renamed Gorkha Parishad. They have since been manipulating the politics of Nepal through their own elements in the Royal Palace.

The Government of India came in for much blame over the Delhi Settlement of 1951 in the post-1951 years. The Nepalis accused the Government of India of betraying the cause of democracy in Nepal. The Government of India had no options available to it. Perhaps one option was the integration of Nepal and India.

Maharajadhiraj Tribhuvan abolished the hereditary rule of the Ranas, withdrew all the powers which his ancestor Maharaja Surendra had given to them under duress, and assumed full royal dignity and power which had been in abeyance for more than a century. He declared that the ministers of the interim government would hold office only during his pleasure and would be responsible to him only. In April 1952, he assumed the title of the Supreme Commander and Field Marshal of the Army, an office that had remained with the Rana prime minister for more than a century. In the pre-Rana period the Maharaja reserved for himself and for his sons the annual *Pajani* (change) of the troops of the chief regiments. The Mukhtyar held the charge of civil military changes. By Special Circumstances Power Act of 9 September 1952, King Tribhuvan invested all executive powers in himself. He promulgated the *Pradhan Nyayalaya Ain 2008* (High Court Act, 1952). On 10 January 1954, he also proclaimed that he wielded supreme legislative, executive and judicial powers in Nepal, and that he alone exercised supreme authority in the country. He thus firmly restored the status of the monarchy as Nepal's polity.

During 1951-55 Nepal pursued a foreign policy identical with India's. King Tribhuvana and Prime Minister Nehru reposed infinite confidence in each other. Tribhuvan even directed his ministers to be in contact with the Indian ambassador at Kathmandu and to go to New Delhi every now and then for consultations. At the request of the Government of Nepal in 1952, the Government of India sent an Indian Military Mission (renamed the Indian Military Training Advisory Group in 1958 and the Indian Military Liaison Group in 1963) to reorganize and modernize the Royal Nepal Army. At Kathmandu's request in 1954, New Delhi assigned Indian military wireless operators to the eighteen Nepalese army check-posts along the Nepal-China/Tibet border. These wireless operators seconded the Nepalese troops and were on Kathmandu's payroll. The Government of India withdrew them both in 1970 owing to an anti-India campaign demanding their withdrawal.

In the belief that India and Nepal had identical

interests in the Himalaya and that they were close to each other in their social ideals and systems of government, Prime Minister Nehru evolved a policy that placed India's northern border at the central ridge of the Nepal Himalaya. A section of Nepalis, however, were not happy with the intimacy between Tribhuvan and Nehru. They particularly resented Nepal's special relationship with India explicit in the provision for joint consultation vide the Indo-Nepalese treaty of 1950. A group under the leadership of Tanka Prasad Acharya even staged a blackflag demonstration against Prime Minister Nehru on the occasion of his first official visit to Nepal. Joint consultation does not necessarily mean dependency. The practice of mutual consultations was in accordance with the treaty binding Nepal and India.

India also advised Nepal to normalize relations with China. On 1 August 1955, Nepal and China established diplomatic relations at the ambassadorial level. On 28 April 1960, there came the Treaty of Peace and Friendship between the two countries, and so on.

King Tribhuvan ended the autocratic rule in Nepal. He ended all such practices as corvee, the grant of land to the government employees in lieu of their salaries, rights and privileges enjoyed by particular classes or persons, etc. He separated the judiciary from the executive. He established the Public Service Commission for the recruitment of personnel to the government posts on the basis of merit irrespective of caste or creed, and so on. Owing to the limitations of time, his revolutionary idea and vision of constitutional monarchy in a yet feudal Nepal could not prosper. It ended with his passing away. Nevertheless Maharajadhiraj Tribhuvan is the second milestone in the history and politics of Nepal created by Prithvinarayan Shah. Maharaja Surendra was the first milestone. Whereas Maharaja Surendra lost the position of the monarchy as Nepal's polity, Maharajadhiraj Tribhuvan restored it. He had intended to democratize the Nepalese system of government and politics. He had intended to endow his nation with a constitution for a constitutional monarchy. However, before he could do this and much else in the social and cultural sectors of his kingdom, death snatched him from the Nepalese nation.

Maharajadhiraj Mahendra Bir Bikram Shah, who succeeded his father on 17 March 1955 and ascended the throne of Nepal on 2 May, constituted a series of governments one after another. By a royal decree on 17 April 1958, he changed the name of the Government of Nepal to His Majesty's Government of Nepal. On 12 February 1959, he proclaimed a constitution providing for a bicameral legislature and a council of ministers responsible to it and making them subordinate to him. The enforcement of the Constitution of 1959 ended the interim period and commenced the constitutional period. Within the framework of the Constitution of 1959, King Mahendra held the first general elections in the country. The Nepali Congress emerged victorious at the hustings and formed the first constitutional government in the country, with B.P. Koirala as the first elected Prime Minister, on 27 March, 1959.

King Mahendra did not find the performance of the elected regime satisfying at all. He warned Prime Minister Koirala of the consequences of the exploitation of the people in the name of parliamentary democracy. Eventually he abrogated the Constitution on 15 December 1960, dismissed the government and jailed Prime Minister Koirala and the other ministers of his government. He dissolved the Parliament, suspended the fundamental rights under the Constitution of 1959 and banned all political parties in the country. Thus the multi-party parliamentary policy, which lasted for a year or so, ended in complete disaster.

King Mahendra ruled directly for nearly two years. He proclaimed a fresh Constitution on 16 December 1962. The Constitution of 1962 introduced the partyless Panchayat system of government and politics called "Panchayat Democracy" in the country. This system differed from the system of party-politics in certain fundamentals, especially in its stress on the decentralization of power within the framework of a three-tier panchayat system with the King and the unicameral *Rashtriya Panchayat* (National Panchayat) at the apex.

The Constitution of 1962 turned out to be a version of the constitution awarded by Maharaja Padma Shamsher in 1947. Maharaja Padma had wanted to hold elections without party support. Introducing the constitution, he had said that the government desired the cooperation of the good, able and energetic representatives of the people but it would be unfortunate "if the introduction of political elections should lead to quarrels . . ." King Mahendra would not even allow political parties to function in his kingdom, etc.

Under the panchayat system the King became supreme. He ruled directly with the assistance of a council of ministers. He appointed his ministers from among the members of the Rashtriya Panchayat and dismissed them at will. All this, of course, upheld the principle of the supremacy of the King in Nepalese affairs.

The entrusting of authority to the village councils to pilot and execute development projects in their respective areas was an important feature of the Constitution of 1962. According to certain sections of opinion in Nepal, the partyless system of Nepalese politics was in line with both the past history of the country as well as its interests. They maintained that King Mahendra created it to balance Nepal's position between China and India. One party politician prime minister might pursue a pro-China policy and another party politician prime minister might pursue a pro-India policy, thereby harming Nepal. And that the partyless system was the sure guarantee against such a contingency.

After the inauguration of the Panchayat system of democracy, King Mahendra made extensive tours of the country especially to bring home to the people the need and desirability of his action. The following extracts from his many speeches at different places are typical of his exhortations:

> Democracy, to speak simply, means that every citizen should get the legitimate right to work for his destiny, nobody should be exploited by any political or social party, everybody should be provided with equal opportunities and justice should be meted out uniformly. Keeping these universal principles in view, the Panchayat system of democracy has been inaugurated in our country instead of the Parliamentary system of democracy whose working had been found to be repugnant to the growth and development of such ideals of human society . . . .
>
> — Bhairhwa, 6 February 1963

> The Parliamentary democracy, to our chagrin, instead of developing the country, almost ruined it and, instead of opening up avenues to the service of the nation, caused sinister schisms among the people. In such a situation, it being also my duty towards the nation to see to the preservation of the country's sovereign, independent existence, to serve the country and the people and to honour and respect the voice of the people, it was not desirable

> to prolong any longer a democracy of mere fun and fashion and a system of government which had thereby proved itself unsuitable to the country ....
>
> —Dhangadhi, 8 February 1963

After installing the partyless Panchayat Democracy, King Mahendra initiated many administrative reforms especially the north-south reorganization of the traditional 35 districts into 4 (later 5) development regions, 14 zones and 75 districts. Besides the requirements of development strategy, the Nepalese Government also intended this north-south administrative reforms to facilitate the movement of the people from the hills to the Tarai. It did this to upset the ethnic complexion in the plains in the context of the Hill versus Tarai politics. Consequently, there has been a considerable shift of population from the hills to the plains.

There is no field, social or political and religious or cultural, which remained untouched by King Mahendra. Social, political, educational and cultural institutions bear eloquent imprint of his ingenuity and acumen. He established the Nepal Association of Fine Arts and the Royal Nepal Academy. He especially championed nationalism and national sentiment in Nepal. He achieved for Nepal the status of a fully sovereign, independent state with well-defined relations especially with China and India, his great neighbours. He broadened the diplomatic infrastructure of Nepal although, owing to financial constraints, he withdrew his resident ambassadors from Indonesia in Asia and Italy in Europe. On 14 December 1958 Nepal joined the United Nations (UN) on India's sponsorship. He was really the builder of modern Nepal, and his reign was one of-construction and progress.

King Mahendra was a poet too. His English poem

"Common Destiny" expresses his royal concern for his beloved Nepal:

We have a common destiny, we
Who were raised from the self-same soil;
As one blood courses through our veins
There's none to claim and none to cast away.

It matters little if you drape
A corpse with course or silken cloth.
Let's fight a battle to the very end
Against poverty, our common foe.

Let's share and share alike
Our joys and miseries,
We'll work together, all as one,
For the land that has given us life.

We shall not cower or cringe
If others raise the sky with rage,
We'll rise as one to save
Our beloved land, our friend.

He who befouls the country's soil
Is wholly dead, however strong he be;
He is alive, though he be dead
Who served his land through love and work.

Crown Prince Birendra (1944-), who acceded to the throne of Nepal on the death of his father King Mahendra on 31 January 1972, proclaimed consciously to pursue the policies of his father and grandfather. As Crown Prince, he had evinced much interest in democratic values. And the liberal views popularly attributed to him then had raised expectations of a genuinely democratic era during his reign. However, it turned out to be altogether different eventually. On the occasion of the first Democracy Day, after his accession to the throne, he paid grateful homage to King Tribhuvan for his love and affection for Nepal and the Nepalis, especially for introducing democracy in the country. To honour King Tribhuvan's memory he renamed the Democracy Day as the "King Tribhuvan Memorial and Democracy Day."

On the occasion of his Coronation, on 25 February 1975, King Birendra Bir Bikram Shah made a comprehensive policy speech. He especially said:

> As heirs to one of the most ancient civilizations in Asia, our natural concern is to preserve our independence—a legacy handed down to us by history. The absence of peace will delay, make more difficult and even deform our development, just as a world without peace will jeopardize our traditional independence. As we are a peace-loving people, we seek to work for peace, not in isolation from the rest of the world, but in collaboration with the whole world. I can assure you that Nepal harbours no ill will or any unfriendly feeling towards any country in the world.
>
> We take pride in the fact that we have close and cordial ties of understanding with our neighbours. If our relations with India have been deep and extensive, our relations with China have been equally close and friendly, consistently marked by understanding of each other's problems and aspirations.
>
> We adhere to the policy of non-alignment because we believe that it brightens the prospects of peace. We need peace for our security, we need peace for our independence and we need peace for our development. As a matter of fact, Nepal in the past had signed formal peace and friendship treaties with both our friendly neighbours. And if today

> peace is an overriding concern with us, it is only because our people genuinely desire peace in our country, in our region and everywhere in the world. It is with this earnest desire to institutionalize peace that I stand to make a proposition—a proposition that my country, Nepal, be declared a zone of peace.

To honour his "beloved father" King Mahendra, King Birendra renamed the Constitution Day as the "King Mahendra Memorial and Constitution Day". On 15 December 1975, he amended the Constitution of 1962, keeping in tact the fundamentals of the partyless Panchayat system. Consequent to a referendum held on 2 May 1980 to choose one option: (1) the retention of the partyless system of politics with "suitable reforms" or (2) the setting up of the multi-party system of politics in the country. The majority of the Nepalis voted for the retention of the partyless system of politics. The amendment of the Constitution on 15 December 1980 introduced direct election to the Rashtriya Panchayat and made the council of ministers collectively responsible to it. It especially enshrined the conception of "Nepal as a zone of peace" in its Directive Principles and also made it the base of Nepal's foreign policy. This so far is the constitutional position of Nepal. The struggle for a system of multi-party politics, however, goes on relentlessly. Even the early and recent bomb blasts, major blasts of their kind in Nepal, seem to be aimed to that end.

Whether or not the Panchayat system reflects the will of the people of Nepal, there is no doubt that it strengthens the institution of monarchy in the country. Now the monarchy is not only in the centre of the decision-making process in the kingdom, it is supreme in Nepalese affairs. Everything concerning the governance of Nepal flows from the Royal Palace. The question, however, is whether King Tribhuvan staked his all for an absolute monarchy or for a constitutional monarchy. King Mahendra was eventually for absolute monarchy. What will King Birendra ultimately be, for constitutional or absolute monarchy?

CHAPTER 6

Nepalese Hinduism

RELIGION—whether animism or Buddhism or Hinduism—has played, and still plays, a great role in the lives of the people of Nepal. It has moulded all Nepalese social norms and values. The grand pontiffs—Jhankris, Bhikshus and Pandits—have also played important roles in the secular affairs of the country. The Raj Guru and the Majhila Guru used to be quite prominent in the political life of Nepal in the early decades of the Gorkha dynasty of Nepal.

The Nepalis, the people of Nepal, are a truly religious people. Besides the great Pashupati and Swayambhu temples of the Bagmati Valley, there is hardly a town or village which does not have a shrine dedicated to a god, goddess, or deity of one kind or another.

Hinduism is the State religion of Nepal. The Hinduism of Nepal is different from the Hinduism of India. Nepalese Hinduism also includes Buddhism, which originally opposed the Vedas, the Upanishads, and the *shastras*, the very source and fountain of Hinduism. Later, Nepalese Buddhism and Hinduism adjusted themselves to each other and learnt to co-exist. Historically the two have peacefully developed together, with no scripture or shrine being burnt down. Since the days of Ashoka, the Hindu kings have always patronized Buddhism. Many eminent Buddhist monks of the historical Nepal Valley became *Acharyas* of the great Buddhist monastic universities of Odantapuri, Vikramashila, etc. Nepal also exercised a strong cultural influence on Tibet through Buddhism. It was from Nepal that Shantarakshita of Nalanda went to Tibet. Many a Tibetan studied under Pandit Buddhashri, Pandit Mahendrabhadra and others of Nepal.

A peculiar characteristic of Nepalese Hinduism is the incorporation of tribal religious elements in its pantheon. Historically, as the Brahmanas and the Kshatriyas spread from the west to east, from the Karnali basin to the Gandaki basin, they accepted the gods and goddesses of the people of tribal origin such as the Kiratas and the Khasas. With tribes like the Magar, the Gurung, the Rai and the Limbu embracing Hinduism during the reign of Prithvinarayan Shah and later, Nepalese Hinduism also accepted in its pantheon the gods and goddesses of Mongoloid origin. The process of Hinduization of the Thakali tribe of Lower Mustang is not complete yet. Nepalese Hinduism has not touched the Buddhist Sherpas so far. Anyway the shrines of local gods and goodesses of indigenous, tribal origin have been and are known as *(s)thanko (s)thani*, "the places/shrines of the local deity". Perhaps it is this which eventually led to the categorization of the Nepalese Hindus as *Tagadhari*, wearer of the thread (the Brahmanas and the Kshatriyas) and *Matwali*, those who do not wear the thread and consume meat, spirituous drinks, etc.

The creater Brahma, the preserver Vishnu and the destroyer Mahesha are, like the Hindu trinity of India, the first gods of the Hinduism of Nepal. Indra, Ganesha, and Kartikeya Kumara are among the other gods of Nepalese Hinduism. Under the influence of the mother cult, the Nepalese Hindus also worship a large number of goddesses whom they look upon as representing the power of the corresponding gods. Brahmani is the power of Brahma: Vaishnavi, of Vishnu: Maheshwari, of Mahesha; Indrani, of Indra; and so on. There are also the deities of other cults and faiths.

Principal among the fierce but benign tantric gods and goddesses are Bhairawa, the War God, and Kali, the Goddess Mother. Both Bhairawa and Kali are aspects of Shiva and Shakti. Of the eight manifestations of Bhairawa, Vatuka Bhairawa wards off the forces of disturbance, whether of gods or devils, in religious rituals and worship. Kali is supreme among all the gods and goddesses of the Nepalese Hindu pantheon. She has many manifestations. Kumari, the Living Goddess of Nepalis also a manifestation of Kali/Parvati. Kali is the first of the ten (10) Mahavidyas. Even rivers, mountain passes and so on have their own Kali like *khola ko Kali, danda ko Kali*, etc.

Of the two major sects, the Shaivites and the Vaishnavites, the former dominate the Nepalese religious scene. Mythologically Nepal is the land of Shiva and Parvati. The worship of Shiva is universal in Uttarakhand, the *Deva Bhumi* of the Hindu tradition. Devotees and pilgrims from India go to Kathmandu to worship Shiva in the Pashupati Temple on the holy day of Shivaratri in the month of Falguna. Even the Rana rulers of Nepal, who pursued a policy of aloofness in order to prevent foreign influences from coming into the country, used to open the borders of their country for a whole month on this occasion. Before the discovery and triangulation of Mount Everest in the middle of the last century, it was generally believed that the peak Gourishankar, named after Gouri and Shankar, was the highest in the entire Himalaya.

In honour of Shri Ganesha, the son of Shiva and

Parvati, ancient Hindu Nepal named after him a whole range of mountains, the Ganesha Himalaya, in its part of the Central Himalaya.

Besides the *Shiva Purana*, which expounds the ethics and philosophy of Shaivism, the Nepalese Hindus except the Ranas rapturously recite throughout the month of Magha a part of *Skanda Purana* called the "Swasthani Brihatkatha". Many, who observe the month-long fast at Sankhu near Bhagau, present to the King the *prasada* of parched maize; soyabean and wheat. This custom has been in abeyance since the death of King Tribhuvan. The *Kumarasambhava* of Kalidasa is perhaps the first Sanskrit poetical work to contain the seed of the "Swasthani Brihatkatha".

The Shivamargi Newars, like the Buddhamargi Newars, worship their tutelary gods and goddesses in accordance with mystic tantric rites. The various aspects of Shiva and Shakti appear in conventional poses and are conceived in terms of their *dhyanas* (meditations).

According to the tradition of Nepalese Hinduism, Gorakhanatha, one of the eighty four Siddhas, founded the Shaiva sect. The Gorakhanatha *yogis* affix the suffix *natha*, which means "lord", to their names. They are distinguished by their pierced ear-lobes from which hang rings of quartz. Because of this, people call them *kan phate sadhus*. They have always had a strong hold over hill culture, though never explicitly acknowledged because of social censure. Cults like the Gorakhanatha cult have certainly had a unifying effect on the hill people not only in Nepal but also in the western parts of the Himalaya. The Gorakhanatha sect is widespread in Nepal with *mathas* in Gorkha, Sallyan, Jumla, Nuwakot, Kathmandu, Banepa, etc. There are non-Brahman Magar priests in some of these *mathas*.

One of Prithvinarayan Shah's most trusted advisers

Ill. 1. Annapurna Range (South side)

Ill. 2. Pashupati Temple

Ill. 3. Goddess Bhadrakali

Ill. 4. Goddess Bhadrakali and King Birendra exchanging swords on the sacred occasion of Dasain/Vijayadashmi

was Yogi Bhagwantnatha of Sallyan. Prithvinarayan had profound respect for him. Yogi Naraharinatha of Kathmandu is now the tireless compiler and annotator of the sources of the cultural and religious history of Nepal.

The festivals and holy days of Nepalese Hinduism are also quite unique. The Nepalese Hindus celebrate almost all the feasts and festivals of the Hinduism of India like Vaisakhi, Ramanavami, Krishnashtami, Dashahra or Vijaya Dashami, Deepawali and Holi. The Vaisakhi festival marks the New-Year's Day of the Hindu calendar. Ramanavami, the birthday of Rama, does not have the same place in the hearts and minds of the Nepalis as has Krishnashtami. Of course, for the Nepalis Rama is the *adarshapurusha*. This is what the *Ramayana* of Bhanu Bhakta in Nepali teaches them. Owing to the message of the *Geeta*, especially Krishna's teaching to stand firm on the path of duty and righteousness, the Sanatana Dharma Samiti of Nepal celebrates Krishnashtami, the birthday of Krishna, on a grand scale. Vijaya Dashami or Dasain as the Nepalese Hindus call it, is the greatest festival of Nepalese Hinduism. The Nepalis celebrate Deepawali to seek the blessings and bounty of Mahalakshmi, the goddess of wealth. The festival of Panchratra, also called Bhishmapanchami, which lasts five days and nights during the dark fortnight of the month of Kartika, is perhaps peculiar to Nepalese Hinduism only. Holi, the spring festival, celebrated during the ten days preceding the full moon of the month of Falguna, may not always herald the advent of the spring season in the Himalaya.

From time immemorial the Nepalis have celebrated Dasain with great zeal as a State festival. It lasts a fortnight from the first day of the Shukla Paksha/bright fortnight of the month of *Ashwina* to the Purnima/full moon of *Ashwina*. During this festival the Nepalis offer their adoration to Nava Durga. It is a joyous festival and is characterized by much feasting. It follows in the immediate wake of Navaratra. On this day the Nepalis receive *tika* blessings from their elders as blessing from the mother goddess Durga Bhawani. They call on each other to express their goodwill. Chaitra Dasain is also a State festival although the celebrations are in much lower key.

Pilgrimage is an equally important feature of Nepalese Hinduism. Centres of pilgrimage include not only the *dhamas* or sacred places of Hinduism outside Nepal like Badrinath, Kedarnath, Haridwar, Ayodhya, Prayag (Allahabad), Varanasi, Mathura, and Vrindavan, but also a number of places in the Nepal Himalaya like Gosainkunda, Muktinatha, Damodrakunda and the other *teerthas* beyond the Himalaya like holy Kailasa and Mansarovar in Tibet. Even now Kailasa and Manasarovara are not beyond their reach. Pilgrimage is an essential part of the *sadhana* of the tantrics.

The temples of Nepalese Hinduism are too numerous to enumerate in this short essay on Nepalese Hinduism. Mention may, however, be made of the Ramajanaki Mandira, the Hanuman Mandira, the Krishna Mandira, the Ganga Mandira and the Pancha Pandava and Draupadi Mandira. Although there is a temple sacred to the Pandavas and their consort, the Pandava legend itself does not seem to have made any impact on the life of the people. These temples are interesting illustrations of the fascinating Nepalese art and architechture—the inner beauty of Nepalese Hindu culture. Besides serving the religious needs of the people, the Hindu temple art of Nepal expresses in a unique way the feeling of religious devotion of the Nepalese Hindu artists as well.

Nepal, an ancient land of an ancient people, has onserved the pristine Hindu traditions, and the culture f the *shastras* and the *puranas*. The interest of the Iepalis since the political change of 1951, however, has ıcreasingly been in things mundane rather than religi-us. And the religious *elite* of Nepal feel deeply con-erned that it may no longer be easy to find people to fficiate as priests in the various temples of Nepal, how-ver lucrative the priestly profession may be. Of course ıere seems to be no problem about finding priests for ıe Pashupati Temple as Adi Shankaracharya, who set p the *matha*, has ordained that they should be from outh India. Even men of South Indian origin born in Iepal cannot function as priests in the Pashupati Tem-le. Nepal and India are politically two different ountries today. Nepal may well decide some day for its wn reasons not to appoint Brahmans from South India s priests in the Pashupati Temple. And if the Nepalese uthorities have found no difficulty in making a change ı the formula for *sankalpa* they may also find no diffi-ulty in not recruiting priests from South India for the ashupati Temple. Any decision to do away with the resent custom, however, is likely to have a historical earing on the future course of Nepalese Hinduism.

CHAPTER 7

Nepal's Relations with Neighbours

NEPAL is an ancient country situated on the southern slopes of the Central Himalaya. In the ancient period it had special relations with the .en cultural world of India, including Tibet. It estaished commercial and political relations with Tibet ıd China in the medieval and early modern periods. It ıd a common border with Bhutan up to 1815. Since the ırly 1950s, its most important relations have been with ; close neighbours, China and India. Nepal and India gned a treaty of peace and friendship in 1950. Nepal ıd the People's Republic of China recognized each her in 1955. Nepal especially reorganized China's vereignty over Tibet in 1956, and gave up all its rights ıd advantages there. Nepal and China also signed a eaty of peace and friendship in 1960.

Relations with India

elations between Nepal and India started as special lations in the 1950s. Since the beginning of the reign of ing Mahendra in 1955 relations between India and epal remained generally strained. Whatever the cirımstances or explanations, Nepal did not side with dia during its military conflict with China in the ıtumn of 1962. King Mahendra had taken the most

serious view of Prime Minister Nehru's comment ("
setback to democracy") when the former abrogated h
Constitution of 1959. Anyway the conflict betwee
China and India did mark the end of the period of speci
relations between India and Nepal.

The fiat of Prime Minister Indira Gandhi—the lib
eration of Bangladesh—more than surprised Kin
Mahendra. It shocked him indeed. He perhaps felt tha
if necessary in India's interests, she might topple hir
too.

Relations between Nepal and India have unde
gone much change. They have suffered from the opera
tion of the factor of common interests, mainly owing t
the differing appreciations of the problems of the secu
ity of the region by the two countries. Nepal is afraid les
too close ties with India should lead to its dominance b
India and compromise its independence. India is wo
ried lest China should gain too much influence in the ke
area of Nepal's northern frontiers. The peace and secu
ity of Nepal and India are indivisible, although thei
approaches are different. There is no natural divid
between Nepal and India. It is, therefore, in the interes
of the two countries to understand rather than misunde
stand each other in the realization of their commo
interests.

The Government of India fixed, vide the trade pro
tocol signed in 1968 a quota for the import of thir
country goods, especially stainless steel utensils and syn
thetic textiles from Nepal into India. Later, on 21 Ma
1969, it imposed a ban on the import of such good
exceeding the quota fixed for them. This sparked
controversy. However, eventually the controversy wa
resolved. Nepalese manufacturers now have duty-fre
access to India on a non-reciprocal basis provided 80 pe
cent of the inputs for such manufacturers are of Indian o

Nepalese origin. There has also been, since 1968, a dispute over the ownership of a forested island, known to Nepal as Susta, on the Gandaki River near Bhainsalotan/Valmikinagar. This continuing dispute too will also eventually reach settlement. Following a shift in the river course, the Nepalese Government laid claim to this 10,000 acre island midstream in the Gandaki. The boundary marker pillars here were washed away several years ago. Both sides admit that the international boundary here runs midstream. In mid 1984 the Government of Nepal urged the Government of India to maintain the status quo in respect of this disputed territory.

An important, if not the most important, element in the relations between the two countries is the border situation. The 1,000-km. long Nepal-India border is traditionally an open border. Occurrence of border incidents of one kind or another, therefore, is understandable. Nepal and India must not allow such incidents to sour the amicable relations between them. The agreement on the control of unauthorized trade between the two countries concluded in 1978 ought to take care of smuggling along the border. Nepal and India are close neighbours: it is not in their mutual interest to become distant neighbours.

Recently certain study groups set up by the Government of Nepal have been contemplating regulation of the free movement of people across the Nepal-India border. Does it mean that the Nepalese Government no longer wants millions of its citizens to travel to India for earning their living? Does it have alternatives for it now? If so, it is great indeed. Unfortunately, it is not quite so. The entire thing seems to be a part of the Nepalese desire to terminate the special relations with India established by the treaty of 1950. Instead of saying that the treaty of 1950 is an unequal treaty, Nepalese Government circles are saying that it is not in Nepal's interest.

Perhaps King Birendra's proposal for the declaration of Nepal as a zone of peace is also meant to circumvent the stipulations of the treaty of 1950. Is not his concept of Nepal as a zone of peace a device for downgrading Nepal's relations with India and for making them comparable to its relations with China? Or is not his proposal to make Nepal as a zone of peace meant to ensure India's non-interference in Nepal's affairs? The Nepalese Government maintains that the proposal neither negates nor obliterates the obligations of the treaty of 1950.

A closed border policy does not seem to be in Nepalese interest. It may not be easy to man a border like the Nepal-India border. It will be financially too expensive to do so. It is also likely to be ineffective. Even the Ranas, who pursued a policy of isolation in order to prevent foreign influences from coming into the country, never closed the Nepal-India border to the people of the two countries. A reorientation and restructuring of the present device of consultation and cooperation between the two Governments can surely lead not only to a more effective policing and administration of the Nepal-India border but also to improvement of the large spectrum of cultural, economic, and political relations between the two countries.

Nepal and India have been close to each other culturally and socially since ancient times. Great cultural and social movements have always criss-crossed their frontiers. At times they have been close to each other even politically. Democracy too, like Sanskritization, is a form of culture. It is, therefore, clear that if Nepal and India are not able to maintain close relations with each other, they should, in the interests of their peoples, at least appear to do so.

India will do well to shed the concept of common heritage or ideals of India and Nepal; for the concept, by implication, equates Nepal's personality with India's. The Nepalis resent this vehemently. Similarly, when the Indians describe the Nepalis as their brethren, the Nepalis do not quite like it. To them it sounds like patronizing. They want to be treated as foreigners, not as brethren. This gives them an individuality and a personality. The Nepalese ambition is to foster a distinct national identity. Their moves to diversify their trade pattern, to change the formula of *arati* the daily ritual of prayer in their Hindu temples especially the Pashupati Temple, and so on have all been motivated by their desire to get away from India. The sooner India stops emphasizing the concept of common cultural and social bonds between itself and Nepal the better for the relations between the two countries. What is called is less of a brotherly and more of a neighbourly attitude on the part of the Indians towards the Nepalis. The fact of common heritage between India and Nepal is important indeed. But it is not as important as the perspective of the national interests of India and Nepal in the contemporary relations between them? In any case a proper understanding and appreciation of each other's national urges as well as interests by India and Nepal may enable the continuity, apart from the rhetoric, of the present pattern of friendly relations between the two countries.

Relations with China

Relations between Nepal and China are quite old. China's intervention on behalf of Tibet in the Nepalese-Tibetan conflict of 1788-92 led to the establishment of China's suzerainty over Nepal. However, the Chinese moves to curtail Nepal's advantages and rights in Tibet vide the Nepalese-Tibetan treaty of 1856 in the wake of the British expedition of 1903-04, greatly perturbed Nepal. The rise of the Chinese power in Tibet in 1951 created much misunderstanding between Nepal and the People's Republic of China (PRC). Nepal at first did not allow the change in the political status of Tibet to effect the special relations between itself and Tibet. Later, in mid 1955, it normalized relations with the People's Republic of China instead of striving with it and established diplomatic relations with it.

Nepal and China in due course discussed the question of the delimitation of their common boundary. On 21 March 1960, they signed in Beijing a boundary agreement on the basis of the recommendations made by a joint commission composed of an equal number of delegates from each side. On 5 October 1961, during the visit of King Mahendra to China, the two countries concluded a boundary treaty. This treaty described the entire Chinese-Nepalese boundary on the basis of custom, tradition, usage, and geographical features. Of course, it made no specific reference to the principle of watershed although it did mention Mount Everest, or Chomolungme and Sagarmatha as the Chinese and the Nepalis respectively call it, and a few other peaks as points through which the boundary between the two countries passed.

On his return from China, King Mahendra said: "By the northern boundary treaty, the Kingdom of Nepal has gained 300 square miles, and I feel that all the Nepalis will experience a sense of glory when I state that Sagarmatha, on which the eyes of the world are focused, continues to be, as it has been, ours and within our territory". Before the conclusion of the treaty of 1961, the Chinese had claimed this highest mountain of the world as a peak of China.

China seems to have been generous to Nepal in the settlement of the boundary question. However, was not China's generosity towards Nepal, as towards Burma in 1960, in the context of its boundary dispute with India? In its anxiety to settle the boundary question, Nepal too surrendered important territories to China particularly Khasa near Kodari, Nepal's present frontier with China, and Rasuwa near Kerung. The northern half of Mount Everest also went to China. The central ridge of the Himalaya did not mark the Chinese-Nepalese boundary everywhere. There were tongues of Chinese territory south of it and vice versa. Border incidents on the China-Nepal border also did not cease altogether as a sequel to the boundary treaty between the two countries.

While King Mahendra signed the boundary treaty, his Foreign Minister, Dr Tulsi Giri, signed an agreement for the construction of a road, to link Kathmandu with Lhasa, with Chinese aid. This raised much interesting speculation then. Commercial traffic between Nepal and China via the Kathmandu-Kodari Highway is not great. There is very little that Nepal can supply to China. The State trading agency, which monopolizes all internal trade in China, also does not allow much profit to Nepalese suppliers.

Not many can equal the Chinese in diplomacy. Even after the establishment of diplomatic relations between Nepal and China in the mid 1950s, the Chinese always said that China would do nothing in Nepal without India's knowledge. Of course, they never missed to emphasize that Nepal should do so without hostility to China. Since the breach between China and India in the latter 1950s, the Chinese have spared no effort to aggravate the discord between Nepal and India.

When necessary, the heads of state and government of China have not deemed it below their dignity to apologize for even ordinary incidents. For example, Zhou Enlai offered China's apology to Nepal over the Kore La, Mustang, incident of 28 June 1960 in which there were a number of Nepalese casualties, including a Nepalese Subedar. Beijing also offered compensation to the Subedar's family and handed over his body to the Nepalese forces on the border. The Chinese leadership also said that the Chinese military contingent had entered into Nepal while chasing Tibetan rebels, mistaking the Nepalese border patrols for Tibetan rebels. Zhou said: "The Chinese troops will withdraw from the areas within twenty kms on the Chinese side of the boundary as soon as the task of suppressing the bandits [Tibetan rebels] had been achieved.

Certain Nepalese assertions that Nepal is a trans-Himalayan country do not necessarily make Nepal a closer neighbour of China. There is no denying that Nepal has tongues north of the central ridge of the Himalaya. The Chhumbi and Pemako valleys of the Tibet region of China also are south of the central ridge of the Himalaya. But that does not make China a South Asian country. Or does it? The Ladakh region of India is north of the central ridge of the Himalaya. Surely this does not make India a Central Asian country. Geographically Nepal and China are neighbours, but in reality they are distant neighbours. Except for the pulls and pressures of power politics there is nothing common in the heritage, social ideals, and systems of government of Nepal and China.

Nepal has a unique character formed and forged by its geographical situation, which is a vital point in the defence of the glaxis of the Himalaya. China perceives India as a threat. India too has a similar view of China. As regards India's position, even a cursory acquaintance with the geography of Nepal is sufficient to indicate that

India's security is linked with that of Nepal. India, therefore, has considerable stakes and considerable interests in Nepal. It can, however, protect these interests only with goodwill and understanding on the part of Nepal.

CHAPTER 8

Prospect

NEPAL is a hereditary monarchy. It has experienced several forms of political transformation like oligarchy and parliamentary democracy as well as panchayat raj, in the two centuries since its creation by Prithvinarayan Shah. Since the introduction of the partyless Panchayat system of politics in the Kingdom in 1962, the Nepalis have experimented with no other system of politics. On the occasion of the 35th anniversary of the Democracy Day, King Birendra delivered an address in which he said that there was no alternative to the partyless panchayat system of politics in the Kingdom.

The political change of 1951 had aroused much hope among the Nepalis. They had dreamt of a truly democratic Nepal. That dream so far has remained a mere dream. There does not seem to be much democracy in the present partyless panchayat system of politics. It only strengthens the monarchy as Nepal's polity.

Nepal has remained a backward state. During the Rana period there was hardly any development in the country. The creation of an infrastructure essential for the development of the country did not interest the Ranas. It was only after Maharajadhiraj Tribhuvan restored the Nepalese monarchy to its traditional position and assumed full powers in 1951 that Nepal was able to take to the path of modernization and development. What will Nepal do next? Will it eventually adopt capitalism or socialism? Absolute monarchy is a barrier to progress. In a country ruled as Nepal is, there is but one source of inspiration—the Throne, where sits Lord Pashupati the King of Nepal worshipped by the Nepalis. The Nepalis also look upon their King as an incarnation of Vishnu. Will King Birendra inspire development, capitalist or socialist or mixed, in his kingdom?

Nepal has a great potential. It abounds in natural resources like forests, mineral deposits, and rivers. Foreign aid, including UN aid, has contributed much to Nepal's development. And yet most Nepalis derive their livelihood from agriculture. Some lead a nomadic pastoral life. Land is the present base for development in the country and land reform is the precondition for both agricultural and economic development. Thus the land reform programmes like the Land Taxation and the Birta Abolition Act of 1959 and the Land Act of 1964, etc., have proved to be progressive measures.

Modernization, especially industrialization, education and social services, has not made much significant advance in Nepal. Industrial backwardness is due primarily to factors such as shortage of capital and technicians and engineers, and to inadequate power facilities. The spread of education has not been achieved for lack of expansion of the infrastructure and meeting the necessary costs. The Tribhuvan University, the Nepal Academy; and certain other centres of higher education and learning serve mainly the Kathmandu Valley. Similar is the case with social services. The establishment of the National Social Service Coordination Council under the patronage of Queen Aishwarya Rajyalaxmi Devi, however, has brightened the prospects for social services and social work in the country. The Queen is a poetess, and, as such, a visionary. How fortunate for the National Social Service Coordination Council!

Nepal has not had much to do with the wide world. Its world-wide contacts first began with the invitation of the Indian Council of World Affairs to attend the Asian Relations Conference held in New Delhi in March 1947. The delegation of the Republic of China, by the by, resented the presence of the Nepalese delegation on this occasion. The Nepalese Government withdrew entry restrictions on foreigners by permitting the first post-war reconnaissance of Mount Everest from the southern side in 1950. Nepal participated in the Afro-Asian Conference held in Bandung (Indonesia) in April 1955. It became a Member of the United Nations in 1955. It joined the Non-Aligned Nations Conference in Belgrade in 1956.

Nepal has taken keen interest in international affairs in the recent decades. Since its admission into the United Nations, it has always cast affirmative vote in the UN General Assembly on vital issues concerning South Africa, West Asia, etc. It has even made its contribution to world peace by assigning a contingent of the Royal Nepalese Army to the UN Peace-Keeping Force in West Asia on 12 February 1974. The Nepalese delegates at the UN have served on several of its committees. What further role it will play in international life remains to be seen. With regard to regional affairs, it can certainly make a significant contribution. It can surely help in the maintenance of peace in Asia. As regards South Asia where Nepal belongs, King Birendra may do well to avoid affording scope for extra South Asian influence in his Kingdom. As the arbiter of Nepal's destiny, he may also do well to reflect why India does not endorse his proposal for the declaration of Nepal as a zone of peace, when China and others have done so.

Appendices

APPENDIX 1

Divya Upadesh*

THIS kingdom is like a yam sandwiched between two stones. Maintain very friendly relations with the Chinese emperor. Also maintain friendly relations with the emperor of the sea of the south. But he is very shrewd. He has been keeping Hindusthana under his control and is now in the plains. He will come in search of forts because it may be difficult for him if Hindusthana becomes united. Keep forts ready in strategical places on the frontier. Put road blocks on the different routes. One day (his) army will come (to attack). Do not be aggressive. Rather allow it to enter. There will be heavy fighting in the lower foothills. Treasure enough for five to seven generations will also be got. Our boundary will also extend as far as the holy Ganges. If (the enemy) is not strong enough to fight he will resort to flattery and various quarrels and deceits.

*The speech of Prithvinarayan Shah made before an assembly of elders, spiritual teachers, priests, relatives and councillors during his last visit to Nuwakot after his conquest of the three cities of the Bagmati Valley and Morang, the kingdom of the *Hindupati*/Lord of Hindus.
I have taken this English version of the *Divya Upadesh* verbatim from the thesis entitled *'Life and Writings of Prithvinarayan Shah'* submitted by L.S. Baral for the Ph.D. degree of the University of London (London) in 1964. I have not made any change in it whatsoever

This kingdom of Nepal is a fort. If he (the enemy.) gains possession of this fort he is sure to subdue all the four emperors. Nepal is a fortress made by God. There is no question about that. Strengthen the forts at these seven places also: Śibepuri, Phulcok, Candragiri, Mahadeu Posari , Paluṁ, Dapoa and Kahulya. In each fort place your artillery and site it according to range so that it commands the road. Wherever there is a pass construct an iron gate in it and at each gate place one cannon and site it so that it commands the road and station soldiers at each of the gates. When this is done such elements as spies, propagandists, absconders, saboteurs, illegal entrants, trouble-mongers, criminals will be powerless to do harm. Even if all the four emperors invade none of them will have any effect at all.

I have seen the social code drawn up by King Ram Śah. I have also seen the social code drawn up by King Jayethiti Malla. I have also seen the social code drawn up by king Mahindra Malla. I had a desire that should God grant I also would draw up a code on similar lines for the twelve thousand (houses). I had a desire to close the routes in the east and west and bring the route through Nepal into operation and prescribe a code for the peculiar duties to be performed by the various castes themselves. This region of the three cities I find to be a cold stone. There is much outward show but nothing else. One who takes water from a well lacks in intelligence and is not brave either. There is outward show and nothing else. I had a desire to construct a palace in Dahacok and build all around it houses for the traditional families and for the spiritual and religious priests, relatives, councillors, military chiefs, commandants and having done that to make my own palace separate. I had a desire to go to the three cities for luxury and recreation only.

Do not permit Indian traders to go beyond God Prasah. If they come to our country they will definitely make our subjects paupers. When we conquered the three cities, the Kirayat yielding an income of nine lakhs (of rupees) and the kingdom of the Hindupati our clothing consisted of Cyaga and Paga cloth. Impose a prohibition on the weaving of Indian cloth. Show samples of Indian cloth to those who know how to weave and instruct them so that they can weave such cloth themselves. The result of this will be that money will not flow into a foreign country. Take indigenous commodities, medicinal roots and herbs to foreign countries and collect foreign currency. Maintain a steady flow of foreign currency into the country. If the subjects are well off the palace will be strong. What is called the treasure of the king is his subjects. Do not farm out the revenue. Collection of revenue is a function of the government. So set up government offices and audit their accounts annually. Do not permit either soldiers of note or relatives and councillors to amass wealth. Give each individual enough to maintain his personal prestige. You may ask the reason thereof. It is because one who is rich will be unwilling to take up arms and kill or be killed. If this happens enemies will become powerful. If the soldiers, my own relatives and councillors cannot afford amenities of life, my sword will resound in all four corners of the kingdom. If they be wholly given up to the amenities of life! . . . This is not a country that I have acquired without great difficulty and hardship. It is a garden of all the castes. Everyone should know that our garden will be a genuine Hindu kingdom for the four castes, whether high or low, and for the thirty-six communities. They must not abandon their caste observances. They must be loyal to the salt of their lord. Do not deprive the descendants of Kalu, the Kavardar, of Kavardarship.

Do not remove the descendants of Śivaram Basnyat from their responsibilities for foreign affairs in the south. Do not remove from the descendants of Kalu Pade their responsibilities of foreign relations with Bhot. Let the Pades, Basnyats, Panthas, relatives, councillors and Magars enjoy authority in rotation. These are my loyal servants, true to my salt and bound by obligations to me. Do not kill them yourself even if they commit crimes worthy of death. Rather invest them with authority and despatch them to battle. If they come back alive, it is well and good. If they die, it is better that someone else should have killed them than that you yourself should kill them. That is why the king should not kill his servant at home. He should pass sentence with complete justice. He should not allow injustice in the country. Those who flout justice and those who give bribe and take bribes. There is no sin if these two types of men are deprived of their property and lives. These are arch-enemies of the king.

The essential thing required by a king is soldiers. Provide them with home and land. They will manure and irrigate it. In this way they will own both shares for themselves. Then their families will have complete security. The soldiers will also be in high spirits whether they be in the capital or at the front. While screening men in the services form a company of hundred guns. As Subedars appoint men who have won reputation in four or five battles and have been examined by yourself. Subedars will also appoint as senior officers seven men who have had experiences in two or three battles. The seven senior officers will choose as non-commissioned officers sixteen men who have fought with them and enrol them in their units. In their respective units they will enrol men of these four tribes only: Sas, Magar, Gurum and Thakuri. One unit should not consist of men of only one tribe. Life will become very hard when fighting takes place. Even the seat of Indra is shaken if one has thousands of bows, thousands of flint-lock guns, thousands of scimitars, thousands of cannon. Both those who fight in battles and those who render assistance are equal. Do not discriminate between them while distributing offices and freehold land. If a man dies give a pension to his son until he is capable of handling a scimitar himself. As soon as he is able to handle a scimitar, promote him to some office. If the king is considerate, soldiers also from different countries will come in hope of reward. If this happens soldiers skilled in swordsmanship will be available. A king's real wealth is his soldiers and subjects. The king should be clever, and he will then keep the soldiers and subjects under his control. So revolt and intrigue will not take place. As regards the soldiers, let him keep them in training. Properly trained soldiers are not likely to be suborned by anybody. Thus his purpose is accomplished. When the Gurums and Magars are away on service, test relatives, councillors, military chiefs, commandants, traditional families to ensure their loyalty and keep those who are old hands with you and in strategical places. Ban the entry of the Sas and Bahuns of the east and west into the palace. You may ask the reason. This is because outsiders create disorder in the palace. Let the king keep all authority in his own hands. I have promoted the Umravas of the three *Thums* to high executive authority and have confirmed them in it. I have given them drums and standards as their insights. I have laid down that they shall each of them receive in perpetuity an income of 240, because wherever they have served on the battle fronts at Sallyan, Liglig and Dhadim, they have been successful and this glorious result has been achieved. Test your old servants of our house, keep them at your beck and call, make adequate arrangements for their duties and emoluments and by so doing keep your house strong. If the king is clever, let him keep his soldiers and subjects under his control. Do not let them to be led into disloyalty by anyone's favour or obligation to anyone. Keep them loyal to their salt.

Ensure that the coinage issued from the mint is pure. In the Court appoint a Thakuri to the post of Distha after trying him. Try a Magar and appoint him as Bicari. Keep one Pandit in each Court and conduct its business in accordance with the customary law and *śastras*. Do not keep the Court money in the palace. Disburse it as gifts and food for mendicants, spiritual devotees, ascetics, hermits, Sannyasis and Brahmans. Disburse the remaining sum as gifts in the form of *dhotis* and scarves. If this happens, the sin which attaches to wrong judgment will not apply. If a mine is discovered in a place where there is a village, move the village to some other place and exploit the mine. If there are houses on arable lands, move the houses to some other place. Dig canals, prepare the land and produce crops.

Once he Ranjit Malla of Bhatgau rendered me assistance. He sent for me but later on he betrayed me. After that with great difficulty I ensured safety of my rear and besieged Nepal. He called naked ascetics from the south to help Jayaprakaś Malla. I did not let them enter Nepal but slaughtered them inside the seven villages. Nabaf Kasmeri San invaded Makuvanpur. I defeated his army with six score swordsmen, routed him and came back after driving him beyond our boundary. Hadi Saheb invaded Siduli Fort with three or four platoons. There I defeated him, captured some flint-lock guns and returned. Three Muslims from Lasanai had come to Nuwakot with a great desire to live under my protection and to be taken into my service. I found that these Muslims knew how to operate these guns. I appointed these three men, Ses Jarbar, Mama Taki Bhesarsim as Ajitans. Thus I had my soldiers trained as riflemen. According to the (history) books of Nepal, it appears that it was to be under the suzerainty of the Turks, Magars and Mugals. It has already been under the Turks. I am the king of the land of the Magars. In order to forestall the sin of its becoming the land of the Mugals I disbanded half of the soldiers of the Thums and formed a Company of riflemen from the other half. Half were trained as swordsmen and half as flint-lock gunners. A Company of a hundred guns is very mobile. In consequence a Company of a hundred guns is the equal of one thousand men. Station one Comapny at each fort and divide them among the Gorsas and keep their granaries full.

I have a doubt of one thing. It is this. The Indian territory is close by. There are boy dancers and prostitutes. (People) may be forgetful of their duties in rooms full of paintings and where there are music, drums and *sitars*. There are great temptations in music. Wealth also is spent lavishly. It is they who carry away secrets of the country also. Consequently enemies will intrigue. Let none indulge in musical exercises. Let none permit the movement of these people into the Hills. Well, you may call one or two for the *Phagu* but send them away quickly. Thus they will not know secrets of the country. For luxury and recreation one may have and see the dances of the Newars of Nepal of the three cities. These dances are sanctioned in the sacred texts. What is given to them will stay in the country. If this happens the country will remain secure .

APPENDIX 2

Treaties

TREATY OF PEACE AND FRIENDSHIP BETWEEN INDIA AND NEPAL, 1950

THE Government of India and the Government of Nepal, recognizing the ancient ties which have happily existed between the two countries for centuries;

Desiring still further to strengthen and develop these ties and to perpetuate peace between the two countries;

Have resolved therefore to enter into a Treaty of Peace and Friendship with each other and have, for this purpose, appointed as their plenipotentiaries the following persons, namely,

The Government of India: His Excellency Shri Chandreshwar Prasad Narain Singh, Ambassador of India in Nepal,

The Government of Nepal: Maharaja Mohun Shamsher Jang Bahadur Rana, Prime Minister and Supreme Commander-in-Chief of Nepal;

Who having examined each other's credentials and found them good and in due form have agreed as follows:

ARTICLE 1

There shall be everlasting peace and friendship between the Government of India and the Government o

Nepal. The two Governments agree mutually to acknowledge and respect the complete sovereignty, territorial integrity and independence of each other.

ARTICLE 2

The two Governments hereby undertake to inform each other of any serious friction or misunderstanding with any neighbouring state likely to cause any breach in the friendly relations subsisting between the two Governments.

ARTICLE 3

In order to establish and maintain the relations referred to in Article 1, the two Governments agree to continue diplomatic relations with each other by means of representatives with such staff as is necessary for the due performance of their functions.

The representatives and such of their staff as may be agreed upon shall enjoy such diplomatic privileges and immunities as are customarily granted by international law on a reciprocal basis:

Provided that, in no case, shall these be less than those granted to persons of a similar status of any other state having diplomatic relations with either Government.

ARTICLE 4

The two Governments agree to appoint Consuls-General, Consuls, Vice-Consuls and other consular agents, who shall reside in towns, ports and other places in each other's territory as may be agreed to.

Consuls-General, Consuls, Vice-Consuls and consular agents shall be provided with exequaturs or other valid authorization of their appointment. Such exequatur or authorization is liable to be withdrawn by the country which issued it, if considered necessary. The reasons for the withdrawal shall be indicated wherever possible.

The persons mentioned above shall enjoy on a reciprocal basis all the rights, privileges, exemptions and immunities that are accorded to persons of corresponding status of any other state.

ARTICLE 5

The Government of Nepal shall be free to import, from or through the territory of India, arms, ammunition or warlike material and equipment necessary for the security of Nepal. The procedure for giving effect to this arrangement shall be worked out by the two Governments acting in consulation.

ARTICLE 6

Each Government undertakes, in token of the neighbourly friendship between India and Nepal, to give to the nationals of the other, in its territory, nationa treatment with regard to participation in industrial anc economic development of such territory and to the gran of concessions and contracts relating to such develop ment.

ARTICLE 7

The Governments of India and Nepal agree to grant on a reciprocal basis, to the nationals of one country i the territories of the other the same privileges in th matter of residence, ownership of property, participation in trade and commerce, movement and other privileges of a similar nature.

ARTICLE 8

So far as matters dealt with herein are concerned, this Treaty cancels all previous treaties, agreements and arrangements entered into on behalf of India between the British government and the Government of Nepal.

ARTICLE 9

This Treaty shall come into force from the date of signature by both Governments.

ARTICLE 10

This Treaty shall remain in force until it is terminated by either party by giving one year's notice.

—Kathmandu, 31 July 1950

TREATY OF PEACE AND FRIENDSHIP BETWEEN CHINA AND NEPAL, 1960

The Chairman of the People's Republic of China and His Majesty the King of Nepal, desiring to maintain and further develop peace and friendship between the People's Republic of China and the Kingdom of Nepal.

Convinced that the strengthening of good neighbourly relations and friendly co-operation between the People's Republic of China and the Kingdom of Nepal is in accordance with the fundamental interests of the peoples of the two countries and conducive to the consolidation of peace in Asia and the world.

Have decided for this purpose to conclude the present Treaty in accordance with the five principles of peaceful co-existence jointly affirmed by the two countries and have appointed as their respective plenipotentiaries.

The Chairman of the People's Republic of China, Premier Chou En-lai of the State Council;

His Majesty the King of Nepal, Prime Minister Bishweshwar Prasad Koirala.

The above-mentioned plenipotentiaries having examined each other's credentials and found them in good and due form have agreed upon the following:

ARTICLE 1

The contracting parties recognize and respect the independence, sovereignty and territorial integrity of each other.

ARTICLE 2

The contracting parties will maintain and develop peaceful and friendly relations between the People's Republic of China and the Kingdom of Nepal. They undertake to settle all disputes between them by means of peaceful negotiations.

ARTICLE 3

The contracting parties agree to develop and further strengthen the economic and cultural ties between the two countries in a spirit of friendship and co-operation in accordance with the principles of equal-ity and mutual benefit and of non-interference in each other's internal affairs.

ARTICLE 4

Any difference or dispute arising out of the interpretation or application of the present Treaty shall be settled by negotiation through normal diplomatic channels.

ARTICLE 5

This present Treaty is subject to ratification and the instruments of ratification will be exchanged in Peking as soon as possible.

The present Treaty will come into force immediately on the exchange of the instruments of ratification and will remain in force for a period of ten years. Unless either of the contracting parties gives to the other notice in writing to terminate the treaty at least one year before the expiration of this period, it will remain in force without any specified time-limit, subject to the right of either of the contracting parties to terminate it by giving to the other in writing a year's notice of its intention to do so.

Done in duplicate in Kathmandu on the twenty-eighth day of April 1960 in the Chinese, Nepali and English languages, all texts being equally authentic.

Glossary

Amban (Manchu),	Governor; Resident Minister.
Antarim Shashan Vidhan (Sanskrit),	Interim Administration Constitution.
Arati,	The daily ritual of prayer and worship in Hindu temples.
Baisi Rajya (Hindi, Nepali),	Twenty-two kingdoms of the Gandaki basin.
Bharodar(N),	One who wears responsibility; a noble.
Birta(N),	Freehold land.
Choubisi Rajya (H,N),	Twenty-four kingdoms of the Karnali basin.
Choutara (H,N),	Platform. *Choutara* (later *Choutariya*), collateral member of the royal family. *Choutarni*, feminine of *Choutariya*.
Chhogyal (Tibetan),	King of *Chho*—righteous law; King who rules according to *Chho* and enforces respect for it.
Gorkhali (N),	Native of Gorkha.
Goshala (S,H,N),	Cow pen.
Gyalpo (T),	King.
Jat (H,N),	Caste; community.
Kaji (Persian),	Judge/Minister
Kashag (T),	Council.

Abbreviation used are S=Sanskrit; H=Hindi; N=Nepali; M=Manchu; P=Persian; L=Limbu; T=Tibetan

Kipat (Limbu),	Community land tenure among the Limbu and Rai septs of the Kirat tribe of the eastern hills of the Nepal Himalaya.
Kothi,	House; dimunitive form of *kotha*.
Lal Mohar (H,N),	Red seal royal decree.
Maharaja (H,N),	Great king.
Maharajadhiraj (H,N),	Great king of kings.
Mahasamanta (S),	Great vassal.
Mukhtyar (P),	Caretaker; Prime Minister.
Mukti Sena (H),	Liberation army.
Mulki Ain (P),	National Act/Law.
Nepal Darbar (H,N),	Nepal Court/Government.
Naya Muluk (H,N),	New Dominion/New Land.
Pallo Kirat (N),	The *trans*-Arun region between the Arun and Tamar rivers, popularly called *Limbuan* on account of its being inhabited by the Limbus.
Panchayat (H,N),	Council, *Gaun Panchayat*/Village Council, *Zila Panchayat*/District Council, *Rashtriya Panchayat*/National Council or Parliament.
Pajani (N),	Choice or selection; annual appointments and screening.
Prashasti (S),	Eulogy.
Raikar (H),	State land-holding.
Raja (H,N),	King.
Ram Shah ko thiti (N),	Code of Ram Shah of Gorkha.
Rana (H,N),	Sept; title.
Rasthra (S),	Nation.
Sabha (S),	Council.

Samanta (S),	Vassal.
Sandejyu (N)	Bull Sir.
Sansad (H),	Parliament.
Sardar (P,H)	Commander; military chief.
Sati (S),	Truthful and faithful lady. Also, custom of Hindu widow sacrificing herself on her husband's funeral pyre; Hindu widow doing this.
Shri/Sri (S),	Auspiciousness, good fortune, majesty, prosperity, etc., also an honorific prefix.
Thakur (H,N),	Lord, also an honorific title.
Wallo Kirat (N),	The *cis*-Arun region between the Dudh Kosi and Arun rivers.
Yuvaraj (S),	Heir-apparent/Crown prince.

Bibliography

Baburam Acharya, *Nepalko Samkshipta Vrittanta,* Kathmandu, 1966.

H.N. Agrawal, *The Administrative System of Nepal,* New Delhi, 1976.

Gautam Bajra Bajracharya, ed., *Shri Panch Prithvi Narayan Shah Ko Divyopdesh,* Kathmandu.

Iman Singh Chemjong, *History and Culture of the Kirat People,* Panchthar, 1952.

M.D. Dharamdasani, *Indian Diplomacy in Nepal*, Jaipur, 1976.

Surya Bikram Gyewali, *Prithvinarayan,* Darjeeling, 1928.

Francis Hamilton (formerly) Buchanan, *An Account of the Kingdom of Nepal, and of the Territories Annexed to this Dominion by House of Gorkha* London, 1919.

William Kirkpatrick, *An Account of the Kingdom of Nepal,* London, 1811.

Percival Landon, *Nepal*, 2 vols., London, 1928.

E.B. Mihaly, *Foreign Aid and Politics in Nepal,* London, 1965.

Tribhuvan Nath, *The Nepalese Dilemma 1960-74,* New Delhi, 1975.

Yogi Narhari Nath, *Itihas Prakash,* 4 vols., Kathmandu, 1955-56.

Chittaranjan Nepali, *Janaral Bhimsen Thapa ra Tatkalin Nepal,* Kathmandu, 1956.

Y.P. Pant, *Economic Development of Nepal,* Allahabad, 1965.

Padma Jung Rana, *Life of Maharaja Sir Jang Bahadur of Nepal,* Allahabad, 1909.

Hemen Ray, *China's Strategy in Nepal,* New Delhi, 1983.

Dilli Raman Regmi, *A Century of Family Autocracy,* Banaras, 1950.

Mahesh Chandra Regmi, *Land Ownership in Nepal,* Berkeley, Ca, 1976.

Leo E. Rose, *Nepal : Strategy for Survival,* Bombay, 1971.

Rishi Kesh Shaha, *Nepali Politics, Retrospect and Prospect,* Delhi, 1975.

Daman Shamsher, *Rule and Misrule,* Delhi, 1983.

Bal Chandra Sharma, *Nepal Ko Aitihasik Ruprekha,* Varanasi, 1951.

W.D. Shakabpa, *Tibet : A Political History,* New Haven, Conn., 1967.

Ludwig F. Stiller, *The Rise of the House of Gorkha,* New Delhi, 1973.

Daniel Wright, *History of Nepal,* London, 1877.

Index